SHORTCUTS TO SUCCESS
ART, CRAFT, DESIGN
PROJECT GUIDE

SHORTCUTS TO SUCCESS
ART, CRAFT, DESIGN PROJECT GUIDE

Junior Certificate

Clodagh Holahan and Maureen roche

Gill & Macmillan

Gill & Macmillan Ltd
Hume Avenue
Park West
Dublin 12
with associated companies throughout the world
www.gillmacmillan.ie

© Clodagh Holahan and Maureen Roche 2002, 2006, 2008
978 0 7171 4116 6

Print origination in Ireland by Carole Lynch
Design by Eilis McDonnell
Reproduction by Ultragraphics Ltd and Typeform Repro Ltd, Dublin

*The paper used in this book is made from the wood pulp of
managed forests. For every tree felled, at least one tree
is planted, thereby renewing natural resources.*

CONTENTS

1. THE EXAMINATION

The art, craft, design exam is based on:

1. a project   75% (300 marks maximum)
2. a drawing examination   25% (100 marks maximum).

The Higher exam consists of twelve parts in total (including the drawing exam). The Ordinary exam consists of a total of ten parts (including the drawing exam).

You will find past projects and past drawing exams in Chapters 12 and 13.

The project

The themes for the project are issued in October (the exact date varies slightly) in the form of an examination paper. The paper contains information and guidelines stating what is required and how it should be presented. The deadline for the project will be in May but you will need to check your paper for the exact date.

You must complete a project that includes:

- 2D studies and preparation (two in the case of the Higher exam – one for painting *plus* one for graphic design)
- support studies for 2D
- 3D studies and preparation
- option (often referred to as 'craft')
- support studies for 3D and option.

A detailed guide to the order of presentation of your project will be found on the back page of your exam paper (see the sample exam papers in Chapter 12).

After the project is completed, mounted and correctly labelled, it is placed in your exam envelope. Once the drawing exam is completed, this work is also placed in your exam envelope and then the envelope is sealed.

The drawing exam

This consists of two parts:

1. natural or man-made objects
2. figure drawing.

Remember:
- Your project carries 75% of the overall marks for art, craft, design.
- The drawing exam in May carries the remaining 25%.

Fig. 1.1
Drawing based on natural objects in pastel.

2. PLANNING YOUR PROJECT

What exactly is facing you?

You are about to start work on your Junior Certificate art project, with a deadline of early May. The project will be based on a theme consisting of a specified number of parts; the number of parts depends on whether you are taking the Higher or Ordinary exam. You will need to map out your work, dividing up your time into six parts:

1. planning your project (the secret of success is to **plan your entire project right at the beginning**)

2. sketching, support studies, finished painting

3. planning, support studies, finished graphic design

4. 3D studies – sketches, support studies, finished piece

5. option – sketches, support studies, executed piece

6. presentation of project, plus extra drawing time.

A variety of themes and approaches are dealt with in this book, but in each section of your project you are only required to produce one finished piece with its relevant sketches and support studies.

Which order suits you best?

You may start your project either with 2D studies (for painting and/or graphic design), 3D studies, or your option. Why not start with whatever section comes easiest to you? For the purpose of this book we shall follow the order of the exam paper layout:

1. 2D studies
2. 3D studies
3. option.

However, you and your teacher may prefer that you start in another area, one that shows your strengths and gives you confidence from the outset.

Here is the (Higher Level) checklist that appears on the back of your examination paper (see also Chapter 12, page 149):

1. preparation for painting
2. completed painting
3. preparation for graphic design
4. completed graphic design
5. support studies for painting and graphic design
6. preparation for 3D
7. completed 3D
8. preparation for option (2D or 3D)
9. completed option (2D or 3D)
10. support studies for 3D and option
11. drawing from natural or man-made objects
12. drawing from human forms.

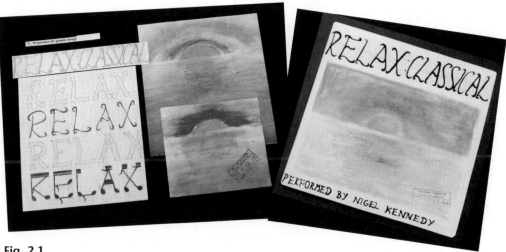

Fig. 2.1
Preparatory work for graphics and finished piece (2D studies).

TIMETABLE

This guide is a rough plan for pacing your project, as the times will vary between the actual date the paper is issued and Easter and the May drawing exam.

Higher	Number of weeks	Ordinary
Planning theme, choosing, etc.	Oct Week 1	Planning theme, choosing, etc.
Halloween		
1 Support studies for painting and graphic design	Nov Week 1	Support studies for painting *or* graphic design
2 Preparation for painting	Nov Weeks 2 and 3	Preparation for painting *or* graphic design
3 Painting	Nov Week 4 Dec Week 1	Painting *or* graphic design
4 Preparation for graphic design	Dec Week 2	Support studies for graphic design and option
Christmas		
5 Graphic design	Jan Weeks 2 and 3	
6 Support studies for 3D and option		Preparation for 3D
7 Preparation for 3D	Jan Week 4	3D
Mid-term	Feb Week 1	
8 3D	Feb Weeks 3 and 4	Preparation for option
9 Preparation for option	Mar Week 1	Option
10 Option	Mar Weeks 2, 3 and 4	
Easter		
Mounting presentation	Apr/May	Mounting presentation
Drawing practice Drawing exam	(throughout the year) May	

Choosing your theme

Choosing your theme is the most important decision you will have to make during the project and you should consider the following questions before making your decision:

1. What is your level of interest in the subject?
2. Will you have easy access to the subject matter?
3. What is the potential for development of the theme within the different exam areas?
4. How much potential is there for meaningful support studies?

Once you open up your mind and your imagination to the themes, you'll be surprised at how the ideas begin to flow. You'll find that all themes can lead you in many different directions.

If the first theme doesn't suit you, you can just move on to the next one. But before rejecting any particular theme, make sure you have thought about it in some detail.

What if you've left it to the last minute?

The first thing is *don't panic!* Panic and worry are a waste of time. Just get down to it and get yourself organised. If you really have left it until the last minute, you should go for something safe. That means something that has the potential for providing you with plenty of easily available objects to draw and get inspiration from. This will help you get down to work straight away. If you choose a theme that allows plenty of scope for more imaginative work, the chances are you'll spend too much time (which you haven't got) 'thinking' about what you have to do, instead of actually doing it.

Beware of choosing one of the more obviously appealing themes, as these can sometimes prove very limiting when you think about them in more detail. The best theme may well be one that initially didn't seem appealing at all. **'Brainstorming'** can help you discover that a theme that seems more interesting on the surface can be quite restricting when it comes to actually doing the project, so be very careful with your decision and look at it from all points of view.

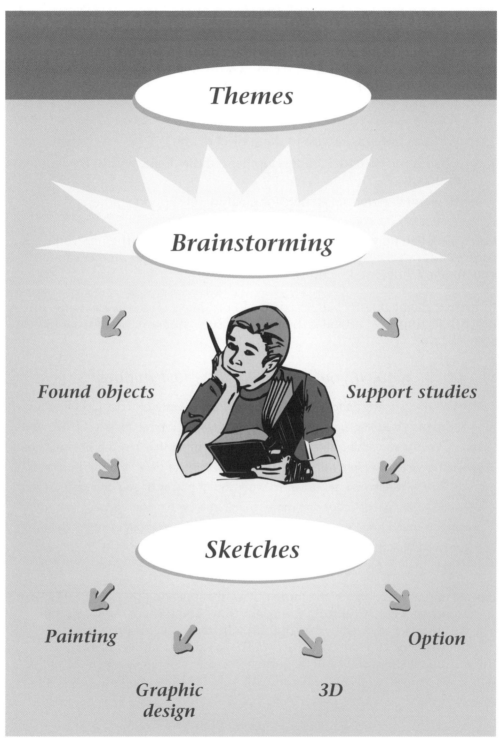

Fig. 2.2
Brainstorming the themes.

Preliminary planning

Plan your time well, then pace yourself. Don't waste time worrying about what you have to do, and try not to leave everything until the last minute.

Most areas in the Junior Certificate need time spent on them, so it's not worth looking for what you think will be an 'easy option'. It might not be the one that suits you or your theme best and could detract from the unity of your project in the end.

Once you have chosen your theme (for more tips, see the section on Approaching Different Themes, page 10), start collecting anything and everything that has any connection to it (see Gathering and Selecting Support Studies, page 13).

While you are collecting your support studies, *draw, draw, draw* anything you can think of to do with your theme. This will not only improve your drawing and observational abilities, but it will also develop the imaginative side of your project, as things can evolve from 'realistic' drawing more easily than from 'pure imaginative work'.

'Preparatory studies are an integral part of the project and must include the candidate's own observed/ imagined images. Mere copying/ tracing is not accepted.'

This is clearly stated on the front of your examination paper.

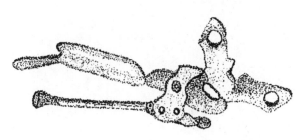

Fig. 2.3
Pointillism (suitable for kitchen/camping/equipment themes).

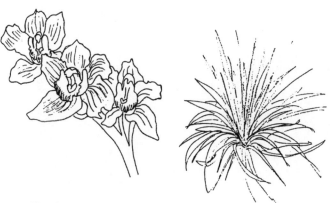

Fig. 2.4
Line drawings (suitable for gardens/ flowers/environment themes).

Fig. 2.5
Cross-hatching (suitable for food/fruit themes).

Take a look at your immediate environment

We all relate best to our own surroundings, or 'environment' – the places where we live, work, study, explore or relax – so why not use your own environment as a starting point? There's no need to feel that you have to think up something amazing or far fetched for your project when in fact your starting point could be right in front of you. All you have to do is to open your eyes and have a look around.

Perhaps you live in the country, in the city or by the sea. We all have different environments that we are familiar with, and interiors – the rooms that you spend time in, like living rooms, kitchens and bedrooms; classrooms, shops, churches, cafés, etc. – further extend the range of environments available to study.

You can develop and explore endlessly in realistic and imaginative ways using and combining any of the vast range of materials that suit your way of working.

Fig. 2.6
A country scene, or landscape. *Note the perspective, the linear quality and the composition in the foreground, mid-ground and background.*

Fig. 2.7
***A water scene*, Leenane (1913) by Paul Henry**. *Note how diagonal lines are used in this composition to create depth and perspective.*

Fig. 2.8
A city scene, showing people and buildings. Note the perspective, the pattern formed by the people, and the general composition.

Fig. 2.9
Yellow Bungalow,
interior by Gerard Dillon.
This painting covers many themes, such as relaxation, people, music, animals/fish, interiors and cooking. In this home scene painted around 1954, Gerard Dillon shows us a typical Connemara family seated around the stove, which forms the heart of the home. Dillon was born in Belfast off the Falls Road in 1916, the youngest of eight children and son of a postman. He is regarded as one of the most imaginative Irish painters of the twentieth century. He died in 1971.

Approaching different themes

1. My bag

Time to brainstorm, brainstorm, brainstorm:

- What kind of bag will you choose?
- What is its function?
- Is it a hand bag? formal/casual/day wear/evening wear/big/small?
- Is it a sports bag? a tennis/football/swimming/running/climbing bag? Is it a skiing/skating/karate/hang-gliding/parachuting/deep-sea diving/go-kart racing bag? Could it be a ballet bag or dancing bag of any description?
- Is it a washbag or a toilet bag/a laundry bag/a shoe bag/a lunch bag/a sleeping bag?
- Is it a shopping bag? a travel bag?

… the list goes on.

Once you've brainstormed to decide what sort of bag you want to focus on, you can do some more brainstorming to discover the scope for inspiration for your project.

Think about the style, the look, the design of the bag and, of course, the contents. Write down all the things your bag holds. It might be a bag designed especially for the items it contains. On the other hand, it might not be the 'ideal' bag for any purpose! It could be a favourite bag, an old worn-out but beloved bag or a bag with character (which might be much more interesting to draw than a brand new one).

Think about what the bag is made of – the material itself, its surface, the texture. Is it canvas, denim, leather, plastic, string, a mixture of materials, or one material pretending to be another?

Fig. 2.10
Shopping bag.

Fig. 2.11
Weekend bag.

HOLDALLS

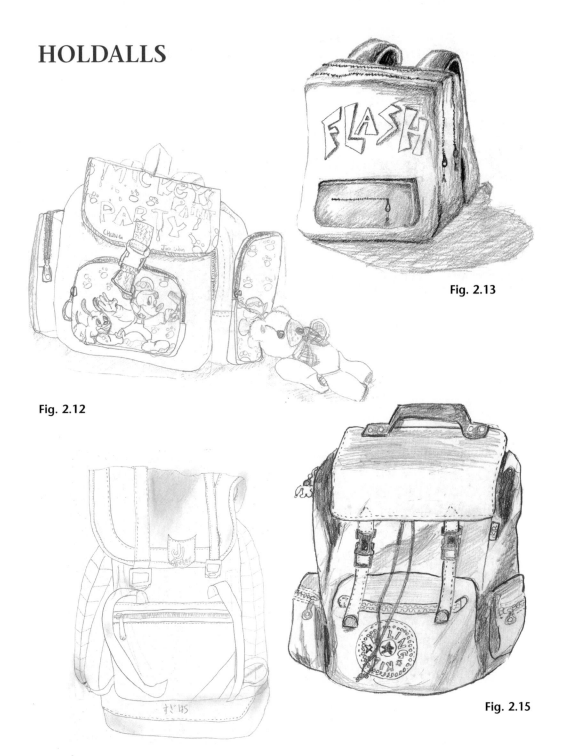

Fig. 2.13

Fig. 2.12

Fig. 2.14

Fig. 2.15

2. My environment – a room/a working room

First, brainstorm all the different possibilities of *each theme*.

Next, 'zoom in' on your *chosen theme*.

Then narrow it down further. For example, you could base your project on the corner of a room, rather than the whole room.

Avoid a project that has too many different elements, which gives a 'bitty' feel to your project, but at the same time, be careful not to let it become boring, for example, the same images appearing with variation only in the technique.

MY ENVIRONMENT – THE ART ROOM

Four different starting points based on the theme 'the art room'; each area allows for plenty of further study.

Line drawings with some texture and tone

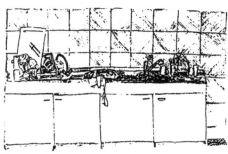

Fig. 2.16

Fig. 2.17

Fig. 2.18

Fig. 2.19

3. GATHERING AND SELECTING SUPPORT STUDIES

Support studies can be any pictures or graphic images that give support to your project and should include a range of visual images that will help you in your approach. Remember that your support studies are an integral part of (that is, not capable of being separated from) your project. They must reinforce what you are doing and relate to it. Your support studies should therefore be collected at the beginning of each section of your project if they are to be of real help to you. For example, when you are choosing support studies for your 2D painting section, you would take the following into account:

- The actual subject matter of your support study should relate to your theme.
- Sometimes an artist's (2D) work inspires you to use the same medium in your work, for example, pastel, paint, collage, mosaic, etc., and your support studies can therefore illustrate a positive influence.
- The artist's composition might relate to the way you are hoping to approach your own painting.
- Your support studies can help you see how another artist approached texture, colour, pattern, or perhaps the time of day or year, in their work.

Support studies are intended to be used to help you in your work. They are not to be added in later as an afterthought.

Continuity is the key word to keep in mind. Your ideas must be seen to grow and develop in some kind of sequence; in fact, that is how most ideas develop. Place all ideas and thoughts on your brainstorming sheets. This kind of thorough planning will create a sound base for your project.

Fig. 3.1
Students sorting out support studies.

The following pages show themes and how they may be developed. The illustrations can be used as support studies.

EXAMPLE: SUPPORT STUDIES FOR MY ENVIRONMENT – A ROOM

Fig. 3.2
Bedroom at Ballylough *(c. 1956), near Castlewellan in Co. Down was painted by Arthur Charlton Armstrong around 1956.* Armstrong was born in Carrickfergus in 1924. This painting shows the cubic influences of Braque, Picasso and Juan Gris. Armstrong spent a lot of time in Spain working and exhibiting.

Fig. 3.3
Medical Students *was painted by Gerard Dillon* while he was living in London around 1949. Medical students were notoriously poor and overworked. We can see that all three are sound asleep during daylight, an indication that they were on duty the night before. Dillon was born in Belfast in 1916. He died in Dublin in 1971.

How should support studies be presented?

Valid material includes any visual or written work which relates to the project and the required area of study, through the chosen theme, from a historical and/or working point of view. Support studies may be either written or visual. They should relate to and reinforce each area of a project or theme. They may be derived from the history and the appreciation of art, craft and design. You may include descriptions of visits to galleries, museums, craft shops and workshops, for example, potteries, foundries, stone-cutters' yards and weavers' sheds. Such experiences may be illustrated with your own photographs or sketches, along with brief captions. Brochures and other back-up materials are also valid. *You must be able to show how your support studies relate to your project.*

Here are some examples of sources of support studies:

- postcards
- packaging (sweet papers to cardboard boxes)
- calendars
- wrapping paper (general/birthday/Christmas)
- magazines/comics
- carrier bags
- newspapers
- book jackets/book promotions
- brochures
- video covers/film advertisements
- catalogues
- record albums/CDs/cassettes
- leaflets
- reference books/books in general
- handouts
- art, craft and design books
- posters
- printouts from the Internet.

4. THEMES

At this stage you should be aware of just how much overlap there is between the various themes, for example, houses/transport, hobbies/pets, movement/sport, nature/environment. Most themes are interconnected and will often involve the environment and people's lives and activities.

The following pages show a selection of images from the brainstorming list suitable for support studies. These images should act as a guide for further research.

Theme: People

Brainstorming list:

- people in their environment, involved in some activity
- cooking/doing the laundry/washing up/cleaning
- eating/drinking (at home, in a restaurant, in a pub)
- sleeping (at home, camping, sleeping rough)
- working (indoors, out of doors)
- at a wedding (inside or outside the church, at the reception)
- at the races/show jumping (an accident)
- a fashion show/behind the scenes
- queuing (for a bus, the sales, for the cinema)
- fighting/protesting (marches, riots, war)
- doing sports/exercise (in the gym, on the pitch, on the beach).

Fig. 4.1
The Discussion *by Renato Guttuso.*

The following pages show a selection of images from the brainstorming list suitable for support studies. These images should act as a guide for further research.

PEOPLE AND WAR

Fig. 4.2
The Shelter Warden *(1942)*
by Thomas A. Crawley. *This watercolour shows the effect of war on the ordinary people of Belfast. If you look closely, you can see a forgotten teddy and a child's shoe at the entrance to the shelter.*

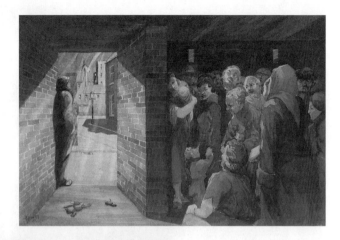

Fig. 4.3
The Execution of the Rebels on the 3rd of May *by Francisco Goya*. *After the Spanish Uprising in 1808, the French arrested and executed rioters and innocent citizens. This painting shows the expression of terror and despair in the faces of the victims.*

Fig. 4.4
WHAAM! *by Roy Lichtenstein (1963)* is from strip cartoons presented on a large scale, so that they take on a monumental appearance. This makes for a strong impact on the viewer.

PEOPLE AND PROTEST

Fig. 4.6
Freedom of Speech (1943) by Norman Rockwell *was one of a set of four paintings used by the War Department in the USA (they originally appeared in the* Saturday Evening Post*). The paintings helped to raise money for war bonds.*

Fig. 4.5
A Fight by L.S. Lowry. *Lowry lived all his life in and around Manchester. He began to be recognised for his work after his first London exhibition in 1939 when he was 51. He worked as a clerk and rent collector in the 1920s and 1930s. Many of his drawings were executed on his rounds, as he would stop and watch any incident, no matter how grim. His figures were much fuller at this time and displayed more detail than his later works.*

Fig. 4.7
Rosie the Riveter by Norman Rockwell (1943) *conveys patriotism and traditional values – it appeared on the cover of the* Saturday Evening Post, *29 May 1943.*

Theme: Shopping

Brainstorming list:

- different types of shops (grocery, fabric, music, fashion)
- food (packaging, displays, supermarket aisles)
- at the checkout (a parent with some children)
- the sales/bargain time (the 'mad dash', queuing)
- window shopping (fashion models, just looking)
- complaints department/exchanging goods
- in the dressing room/trying on shoes/picking a CD
- buying a bicycle/a motorbike/a car
- a coffee break/meeting friends (with all the bags and packets)
- the salesperson (in a shop, on the doorstep, in the garden centre).

Fig. 4.8
Photo by Gerard Fritz.

The following pages show a selection of images from the brainstorming list suitable for support studies. These images should act as a guide for further research.

MEAT MARKET

Fig. 4.9
Smithfield Market *by Beryl Cook.* Beryl Cook is one of Britain's most famous contemporary artists. Much of her work is published in books and on greeting cards. Her subject is always people and their various activities. Her people are well rounded, full of life and humour. This early morning picture shows the beef and lamb carcasses in Smithfield Market. We see the bustle of activity of the porters as they move great sides of beef into their various rows.

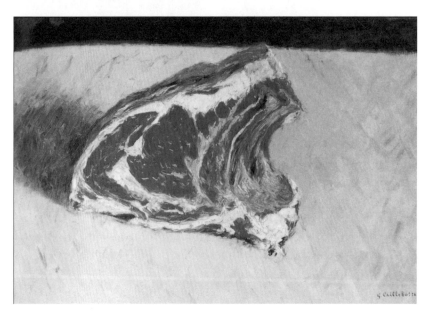

Fig. 4.10
Rib of Beef (Côte de Boeuf) *by Gustave Caillebotte (1882).* This painting is a still-life-type study of a rib of beef using a soft-toned 'Impressionist' palette.

HOLIDAY SHOPPING

Fig. 4.11
Harrods *by Beryl Cook*. *In this painting, Cook shows an enterprising man who is doing a tap-dance outside the famous Harrods store. His radio and hat can be seen on the ground. Judging by the contents of the hat, he is having a profitable day. Being in Knightsbridge, the ladies would naturally be very stylishly dressed. The lady with the hat in the foreground is wearing an outfit borrowed from the late Princess Diana's wardrobe.*

Fig. 4.12
Photo by Jose L. Pelaez. On holiday or being a tourist usually suggests casual clothes and comfortable shoes. Most tourists have a camera ready at hand for that special, not-to-be-missed holiday photograph.

Theme: Spare time/hobbies/relaxing

Brainstorming list:

- relaxing (listening to music, reading, watching TV, gardening)
- talking (gossiping, chatting on the phone)
- board games (chess, draughts, dice games, jigsaws)
- playing cards (bridge, poker, solitaire)
- holidaying (sightseeing, sunbathing, walking, fishing)
- visiting friends (coffee, lunches, dinner)
- amusements (arcades, fairgrounds, festivals)
- computers (cybercafés, surfing the net, games)
- art and craft work (painting, weaving, photography, sewing)
- pets (cats, dogs, rabbits, turtles, birds).

Fig. 4.13
Les Joueurs de Cartes (The Card Players, 1890–97) by Paul Cézanne (1839–1906).

The following pages show a selection of images from the brainstorming list suitable for support studies. These images should act as a guide for further research.

RELAXING

Fig. 4.14
Perspective is enhanced by the lines in the sand.

Reflected sunlight always creates marvellous effects. Observe the linear patterns in the sand and on the young woman's skirt.

Fig. 4.15
Light Falls Within *(1978)* **by Carol Graham**. *Carol Graham was born in Belfast in 1951. Her paintings use a form of photorealism in which she shows light shining through fabric. More recently she has achieved success as a portrait painter, having painted former President Mary Robinson for Trinity College Dublin.*

Fig. 4.16
Laid-back and relaxed. Lost in his own world, this musician lets time drift by.

RELAXING, READING, SEWING

Fig. 4.17
Photo by Jose L. Pelaez.

Fig. 4.18
La Liseuse *by Mary Cassatt,*
one of the few women
Impressionists (an American).

Fig. 4.19
Vanessa Bell *by*
Duncan Grant.

Fig. 4.20
The Red Hammock (*1936*) *by Sir John Lavery*.
Lavery was born in Belfast in 1856 and died in Kilmoganny,
Co. Kilkenny in 1941. He painted many pictures of his
beautiful American wife, Hazel. He is known mainly for his
portraits, one of the most famous being the portrait of his
wife on the Irish Pound Note. Her portrait was also seen as
a watermark on the Irish punt.

Fig. 4.21
The Girl in the Window *by Harry Morley*.

PETS

Fig. 4.22
Cat on Mat *by Jack P. Hanlon.*

From an unusual perspective

Fig. 4.23
A Couple of Foxhounds *painted in 1792 by George Stubbs (1724–1806).*

Fig. 4.24
Man's best friend.

Fig. 4.25
UNICEF card illustration, Martin Leman (UK). *Clear shapes, nature in plant and animal form.*

Theme: *Horses*

Brainstorming list:

- horses
- equipment to do with a horse (saddle, bridles, reins)
- pets (looking after a horse, the food a horse eats)
- circus (performing horses in the ring or on parade)
- hobby/entering competitions (learning to ride, entering events)
- happiness (winning a horse event, racing or jumping)
- on the farm (the horse as a work animal)
- folklore (legends about horses)
- transport (horses pulling beer barrels, scrap merchants)
- movement (the way a horse moves/rears/kicks).

Fig. 4.26
For the Road *by Jack B. Yeats.*

The following pages show a selection of images from the brainstorming list suitable for support studies. These images should act as a guide for further research.

HORSES

Fig. 4.27
Mares and Foals in a River Landscape *by George Stubbs (1724–1806). Stubbs painted horses in great detail. He studied anatomy and science as well as being a masterly painter of animals.*

Fig. 4.28
Race Horses at the Grandstand *by Edgar Degas (1834–1917). Races could also come under hobbies.*

Fig. 4.29
The Blank Signature (1965) by René Magritte (1898–1967). *This picture could also be suitable for the themes of nature/trees or dreams.*

Fig. 4.30
The Tower of Blue Horses *by Franz Marc (1880–1916). Roughly painted, showing great movement and style.*

DEATH AND THE HORSE

Fig. 4.31
This woodcut by Albrecht Dürer (1471–1528), called Knight, Death and Devil was printed in 1513. *A woodcut is a way of producing a picture using the principles of printing.*

Fig. 4.32
William Blake (1757–1827) *was both an artist and a poet. His vision was unique and he conveyed his restless spirit in an unusual and very graphic manner. In* **Death on a Pale Horse – The Fourth of the Apocalypse,** *Blake shows the spirit locked in combat between good and evil.*

Theme: Sport

Brainstorming list:

- team games (football, hockey, hurling, camogie, soccer, rugby, baseball, cricket, basketball)
- partner games (tennis, squash, handball, badminton)
- solo sports (running, high jump, golf, ice skating, skiing, trampoline, gymnastics, biking, horse riding, swimming)
- equipment (clothes, shoes, rackets and balls)
- pitches/courts/ice rinks/tracks/snow slopes/pools
- changing rooms/behind the scenes/training
- supporters/flags/mascots/rosettes
- sponsorship/advertising
- injuries/fouls/accidents
- contests/winning/trophies/presentations.

Fig. 4.33
A determined Lleyton Hewitt lunges for a volley on his way to winning the Men's Final at Wimbledon.

The following pages show a selection of images from the brainstorming list suitable for support studies. These images should act as a guide for further research.

SCRAMBLING AND RACING

Fig. 4.34

Fig. 4.35

Fig. 4.36

Stamps:
Isle of Mann TT races – Irish winners

Fig. 4.37

Fig. 4.38

On 30 May 1996, four commemorative stamps, three of which are shown above, were issued by An Post to celebrate the achievements of Irish riders in the Isle of Man TT races over its ninety-year history. The stamps were designed by Joe Dunne and featured some of our most celebrated riders, including Stanley Wood (32p), Artie Bell (44p), Alec Bennett (50p) and Robert and Joey Dunlop (52p).

Fig. 4.39
All shoes make interesting subject matter for drawing, but sports shoes provide a great variety of line and shape, as this repeat pattern shows.

Theme: Nature

Brainstorming list:

- trees/forests/woodlands (branches, twigs, undergrowth)
- greenery/leaves (different shapes, patterns, colours)
- flowers/wild and cultivated animals (bees, butterflies)
- lanes/country walks (mud tracks, puddles, footprints)
- land/fields (fences, hedges, gates, skies, grass, corn)
- wild animals/birds (foxes, rabbits, squirrels, ducks)
- pollution in the countryside (rubbish dumps, blocked rivers)
- waterways/rivers/streams/lakes (reflections, movement)
- farms, mixed organic farms, working closely with nature
- country houses/garden sheds.

Fig. 4.40
November Morning *by Maureen Roche, screen print.*

The following pages show a selection of images from the brainstorming list suitable for support studies. These images should act as a guide for further research.

TREES

Fig. 4.41
Trees are wonderful on their own, but when a background is added, it gives them a sense of belonging and can create depth.

Fig. 4.42
La Ferme de Lézavier, Finistére *by Roderic O'Conor (1860–1940)*. *Oil on canvas.*

Fig. 4.43
Dorset Chalk Quarry *by Harry N. Morley.*

FLOWERS

Fig. 4.44
Two Calla Lilies on Pink *(1928)* by
Georgia O'Keeffe *(1887–1986)*. *O'Keeffe's*
work could fit into many categories,
including precisionism, surrealism and/or
modernism. She works on a large scale and
presents clear and simple images covering a
wide range of subjects.

Flowers are all around us. They are used to beautify our streets and houses. They are a very acceptable gift and their arrangement can be an artform in itself.

Fig. 4.45
Flower Arrangements *by students*.

Fig. 4.46
Crocuses.

Fig. 4.47
Flowers *by Jack Hanlon*
***(1913–1968)*.** *One of many*
Irish artists to study under
André Lhoté in Paris. This
painting of flowers contains
elements of cubism.

CATS AND DOGS

Fig. 4.48
Three Cats *by Elizabeth Blackadder, RA.*

Fig. 4.49
Cat at the Ready *by Clodagh Holahan.*

Fig. 4.50
Studies of Cats *(1992) by John Ward, RA.*

Pets are wonderful to draw, as most people have an emotional attachment to them (see also page 25).

Fig. 4.51
Detail from **Cape Cod Evening** *by Edward Hopper (1882–1967).*

Theme: Entertainment

Brainstorming list:

- venues (theatres, cinemas, concert halls, opera houses)
- music (musical instruments, musicians)
- orchestras/bands/groups (traditional, classical, pop, jazz)
- singing (singers, backing groups, microphones, lighting)
- TV/films/cameras/sets/location/film crews
- dance (dancing shoes, costumes, ballet, folk, discos, cafés)
- parades (brass bands, dancing)
- circuses/ice rinks/sports (spectators, participants)
- comedy (magic, clowns, parties, cabarets)
- grand openings/celebrations (Olympics, World Cup).

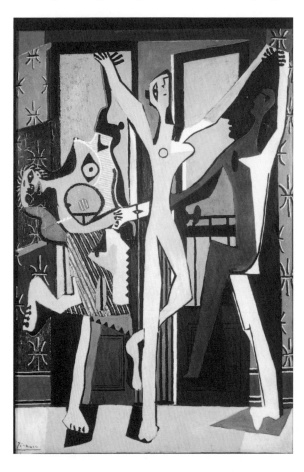

Fig. 4.52
Three Dancers *by Pablo Picasso (1881–1973).*

The following pages show a selection of images from the brainstorming list suitable for support studies. These images should act as a guide for further research.

MUSIC/MUSICAL INSTRUMENTS/CELLOS

Fig. 4.53
Cellomaster *by Arman (born 1928)*. *This cello has been 'rhythmically' dissected and carefully put back together. Arman loves music and the shape of some musical instruments, which remind him of women.*

Fig. 4.54
Portrait of a Young Woman *by Meredith Frampton*. *The cello forms part of the setting for this portrait.*

Fig. 4.55
Quintet *by Raoul Dufy*. *Through this rather sketchy painting you can feel the music and the action of the players.*

TV/FILMS/COMPUTERS

Fig. 4.56
Watching TV by Tsing-Fang Chen. In the picture, the audience has been borrowed from Vincent Van Gogh's The Potato-Eaters.

TV and computers have changed peoples home lives completely.

Fig. 4.57
Modern Madonna by Christian Pierre.
If Jesus was born today, would he find himself in this environment?

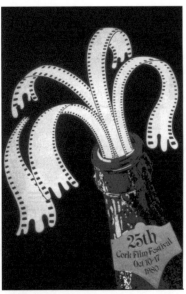

Fig. 4.58
Films entertain, but they also reflect our culture. Film festivals and openings are reasons for celebration, marked with the opening of champagne bottles – this poster for the Cork Film Festival from Limerick Art College captures this very well.

Theme: Fantasy

Brainstorming list:

- monsters/masks/costumes
- outer space/creatures from outer space
- weird weather conditions
- dragons
- stories from mythology and legend
- mermaids/underwater wonders
- nightmares/distorted images/ghosts
- witches/wizards/druids/spells
- fairies/elves/leprechauns
- films/cartoons/theatre/puppets.

Fig. 4.59
Fantasy can best be defined as an idea not based on reality – it is unreal, unbelievable.

The following pages show a selection of images from the brainstorming list suitable for support studies. These images should act as a guide for further research.

FANTASY ART – SURREALISM

Surrealism shows the activities of the unconscious mind – a dream-like world.

Fig. 4.60
Elohim Creating Adam (c. 1805) by William Blake. *Blake is not considered a surrealist artist, but his work definitely shows surreal qualities.*

Fig. 4.61
Les Amants *by René Magritte.*

Fig. 4.62
The Lament for Icarus (1898) by Herbert J. Draper (1863–1920).

Fig. 4.63
La Découverte du Feu *by René Magritte.*

Fig. 4.64
Because bats are nocturnal, they are often associated with ghosts and vampires.

René Magritte was a member of the surrealist movement. His subject matter is treated in a very realistic way, but it is the manner in which he composed his paintings that gives a surreal quality to the work.

FANTASY – DEPICTING ANIMALS

Fig. 4.65
The Unbidden *by R. Chetwynd Fayes.* *The fantasy in this picture comes from combining a realistic head with fantasy snakes. The intertwined snakes represent evil and destruction.*

Fig. 4.66
Raiders of Gor *by John Norman.* *The brave hero travelling on the back of a bird is a feature of many myths and legends throughout the world.*

Theme: Buildings

Brainstorming list:

- in the city/in the country (farms, barns)
- houses/apartments/interiors
- churches/funeral homes
- town halls/civic buildings
- offices/factories/airports
- hospitals/nursing homes/sheltered accommodation
- schools/universities/parliament buildings
- police stations/fire stations/court houses/prisons
- theatres/concert halls/opera houses
- castles/towers/ruins (rural, urban, old-fashioned, modern, different styles).

Fig. 4.67
Gandons's Customs House, Liberty Hall and River Liffey, Dublin. *The new and the old – one vertical, the other horizontal alongside the river.*

The following pages show a selection of images from the brainstorming list suitable for support studies. These images should act as a guide for further research.

DWELLING HOUSES

Fig. 4.68

Irish Cottage, Feakle, Co. Clare*. The traditional Irish cottage made a big 'comeback' as a tourist attraction in the late 1960s. The local people preferred their new bungalows as the cottages held bad memories of poverty and hard living, unlike the newly built cottages for the tourist, which possessed all the mod cons of the time, including central heating.*

Fig. 4.69

The Red House at Bexley Heath in Kent*, which was specially designed for William Morris by Philip Webb in 1859. William Morris (1834–1890), the famous English designer of fabrics and wallpaper, lived in great style in the Red House.*

CHURCHES

Church architecture changed dramatically in the twentieth century.

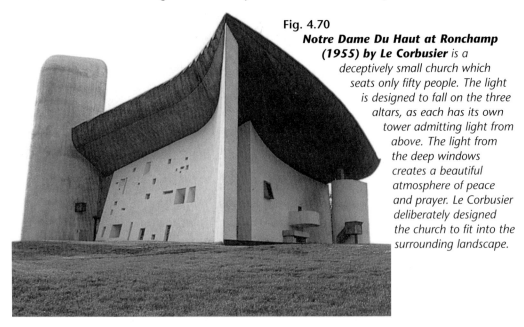

Fig. 4.70
Notre Dame Du Haut at Ronchamp (1955) by Le Corbusier *is a deceptively small church which seats only fifty people. The light is designed to fall on the three altars, as each has its own tower admitting light from above. The light from the deep windows creates a beautiful atmosphere of peace and prayer. Le Corbusier deliberately designed the church to fit into the surrounding landscape.*

Fig. 4.71
*Changes in the Catholic religion in the early 1960s greatly affected church architecture. Old churches were renovated and new ones were built, like **St. Angus Burt, Co. Donegal by Liam McCormach (1967)**. Sometimes the altar was brought down into the main body of the church and, because of this, churches adopted a circular shape.*

Theme: Food

Brainstorming list:

- sources (farming, animals, sea)
- crops/fruit trees/kitchen garden/greenhouses
- harvest time (gathering food, hunting, fishing, storing)
- market/wholesalers/shops/hot-dog stands
- cooking/baking/kitchens (at home, in hotels, in hospitals)
- cakes (special occasions, including birthdays and weddings)
- specialist cooking (vegetarian, fish, meat)
- foreign foods/restaurants (Italian/spaghetti, Chinese/rice)
- cooking on an open fire (camping, barbecues, picnics)
- ice cream (ice cream parlours, at the seaside, in the streets, ice cream vans).

Fig. 4.72
Freedom from Want (1943) by Norman Rockwell.

The following pages show a selection of images from the brainstorming list suitable for support studies. These images should act as a guide for further research.

HARVEST TIME: GATHERING/STORING

Fig. 4.73

Fig. 4.74
Nuts, lentils, corn, pasta, beans and rice are all very popular in modern diets.

Fig. 4.75
Nowadays most of the fruit and vegetables we eat are on the supermarket shelves within a few hours of being harvested. The produce often comes from different countries and can vary depending on the season.

SPECIALIST COOKING

Fig. 4.76
*Here we see a chef with a beautiful selection
of afternoon-tea treats.*

Fig. 4.77
*This lavish buffet has a vast variety of fish and
meat dishes, accompanied by cheese and grapes.
Note the two seahorses made of ice in the
background.*

Fig. 4.78
*Christmas is probably the best time of the year for specialist cooking. Cakes,
puddings, mince pies, turkey, stuffing, roast potatoes and loads of vegetables
all add up to making the festive holiday more memorable.*

Theme: Transport

Brainstorming list:

- land, sea (including underwater), air (including space travel)
- boats (sailing boats, canoes, rafts, motorboats, cruisers, lifeboats)
- trains (high-speed, steam, wild west, cargo trains)
- cars (vintage, sports, saloon, racing)
- aeroplanes (passenger planes, sea planes, fighter jets, Concorde)
- bicycles (mountain bikes, racing bikes, tandems, penny-farthings)
- motor bikes (racers, Harley Davidsons, 'easy riders')
- horse-powered (carriages, ponies and traps, cart horses)
- buses, coaches, lorries, vans, juggernauts, cable cars, lifts
- wheelchairs, prams, baby buggies, escalators, moving ramps.

Fig. 4.79
Busy street with Dublin Tour Bus.

The following pages show a selection of images from the brainstorming list suitable for support studies. These images should act as a guide for further research.

CARS

Fig. 4.80
Long-Term Parking (1982). *The artist **Arman** took fifty-nine brightly coloured cars (Buicks, Renaults and Citröens) and parked them for eternity in 1,600 tons of concrete, making a sarcastic monument to our consumer society. It is approximately 20 metres high and 6 metres wide. Arman is known for his accumulations. He has assembled piles of saws and coffee-pots and even rubbish. The long-term parking monument has annoyed residents living nearby as they fear it could devalue their property.*

Fig. 4.81
Universe Hearse – Play Now Rest Later (Motto). *Some old cars are treasured, even if their original function has been changed, as in this hearse with the motto 'Play Now, Rest Later.' People have been invited to engrave their 'words to live by' on 30,000 individual mosaic pieces of Plexiglas.*

BOATS/SHIPS

Fig. 4.82
When viewed from below, these giants of the sea look extremely impressive. Advertisers used this trick to show the power of such ships and to emphasise their size.

Fig. 4.83
The Arrival *by Christopher Nevinson still keeps that powerful angle. Though treated in an abstract manner, it strongly suggests embarking at a port.*

Fig. 4.84
Barge at Edenderry *(1936), a peaceful scene through still waters by Romeo Charles Toogood (1902–1966).*

TRAINS

Fig. 4.85
Future Train *by Alan Carver*. *Some trains are taking on a space-age look as they are streamlined to go increasingly faster.*

Product code 9505MS

Fig. 4.86
These stamps, designed by Charles Rycraft, *show steam engines that served different locations in Ireland long ago.*

Fig. 4.87
Night Train *by Paul Delvaux (1897–1994)*. *The night seems to emphasise the loneliness that often follows the departure of a train (note the young girl at the bottom right).*

5. PUTTING TOGETHER A SUCCESSFUL PROJECT

A successful project should be visually interesting as well as competent. Your initial feelings about the first stages of your project or theme can be very strong and it is important that you communicate this strength of feeling in your work. Never assume that the examiner knows what you are trying to do. Explain yourself clearly; show off your knowledge.

If you are stuck for space, carefully choose what to include and what to leave out.

Fig. 5.1

Fig. 5.2

To arrive at this final study, the student first made separate studies of the individual components of the picture, concentrating on **pattern, colour and line** and the relationships of **shapes and textures**.

It is important to remember that preparatory work (which includes preparation development and support studies) carries 66% of the marks, whereas the finished work carries 33%.

On the following pages are samples from a variety of successful projects.

THEME: FOOD

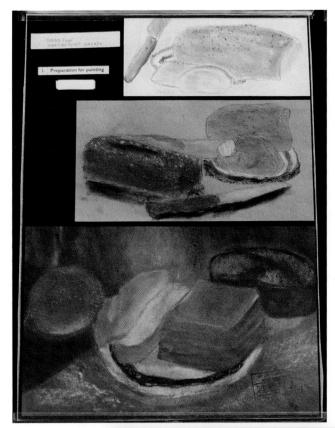

Fig. 5.3
Three preparatory student sketches for the theme of food.

A corner gives a stabilising effect and makes for an interesting composition, with a variety of tone.

Fig. 5.4
Completed painting, *with all the work carried out in pastel.*

THEME: RELAXING

Painting

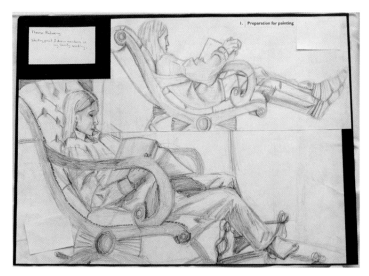

Fig. 5.5
Preparation for painting*. Student's note (top left) reads: 'Theme – Relaxing. Starting point:
I drew members of my family reading.'*
*This is a good example of preparation work. The student has viewed the chair and person from
two different angles, showing an understanding of perspective and the proportions of the
figure. Perhaps it is a little overworked and slightly limited in technique and media,
but it demonstrates good, strong preparatory work.*

Fig. 5.6
Completed painting using pastels.

THEME: RELAXING

Graphic design

Fig. 5.7
Preparation for graphic design.
In this preparatory work, the measurement and spacing are clearly visible. Perspective is evident in the drawing of the figure, giving an isolating effect to the reader absorbed in his book.

Fig. 5.8
Completed graphic design.
The final work shows a clear, legible notice, fulfilling the function of a poster.

Fig. 5.9
Support study sheet for 3D and option.

THEME: RELAXING

3D

Fig. 5.10
Preparation for 3D.

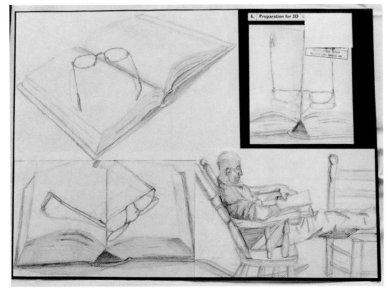

The student zoomed in on the book and spectacles of the man relaxing. They then became the focal point for the 3D piece. The perspective problems encountered in the preparatory drawing were resolved once the piece was translated into 3D format.

Fig. 5.11
Completed 3D (clay, wire and plaster).

The subject often dictates the materials you should use, for example, the wire in the glasses, whereas the book was easily modelled in clay.

THEME: RELAXING

Support studies for painting and graphic design

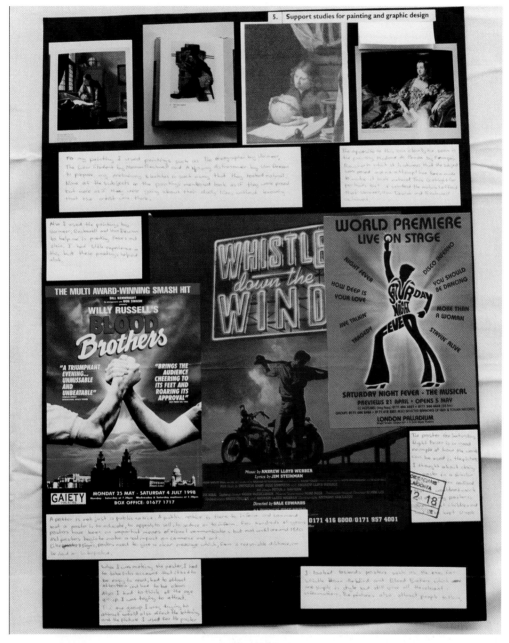

Fig. 5.12
*A good example of a support studies sheet with a balance of written and visual images showing
a range of art and graphic examples. Typing is definitely clearer and easier to read,
though it does lack that personal touch.*

THEME: FOOD

Painting

Fig. 5.13
Preparation for painting. *Starting point: Cows and milk.*

*The student used their own environment as a starting point for the theme of food,
choosing pencil and paint and zooming in on the cow and calves for the composition.
This sheet shows the preparation and development of the theme from the starting point.*

Fig. 5.14
Completed painting. *The finished painting shows a definite contrast of colour and texture.*

THEME: FOOD

Graphic design

Fig. 5.15
Preparation for graphic design.

Lots of preparation work with block lettering using a grid.

Fig. 5.16
Completed graphic design.

The lettering and the diagonal image of the cow are linked, giving an interesting impression of continuity which holds the poster together.

Fig. 5.17
Support studies for 3D and option (batik).

THEME: FOOD

Support studies for painting and graphic design

This page of support studies shows a variety of successful graphic examples together with a range of artwork and relevant commentaries.

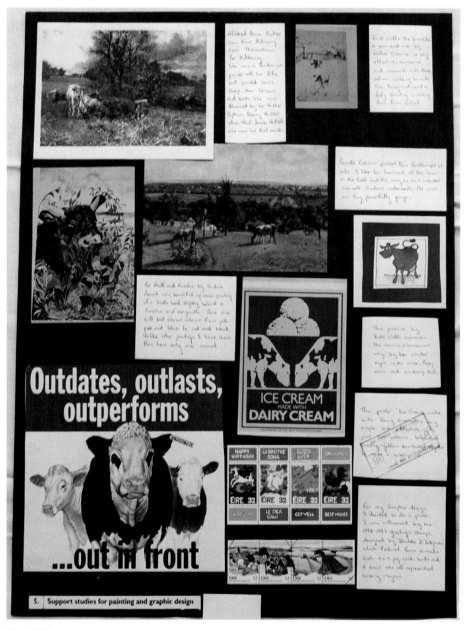

Fig. 5.18

THEME: MUSIC

Graphic design

A study of a boot was developed into a design for the CD cover 'Journey into Death'.

Fig. 5.19

Fig. 5.20

THEME: ENVIRONMENT

Fig. 5.21
Preparation for graphic design.

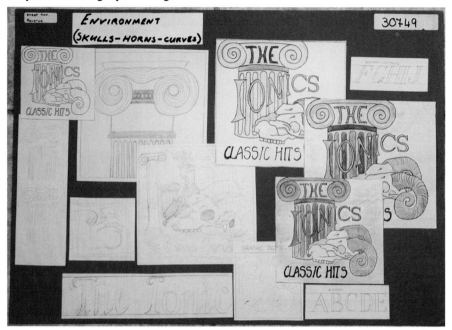

Fig. 5.22
Graphic design.

The student narrowed down the theme of environment to a sheep's skull. The curve of the sheep's horns suggested a relationship with Ionic columns and so the project developed.

Record sleeve/CD cover. Studies of lettering and the subject matter lead to the name on the record sleeve, 'The Ionics'. The student experimented with different colour combinations once the layout was worked out.

THEME: ENVIRONMENT

Fig. 5.23
***Preparation for 3D**.*

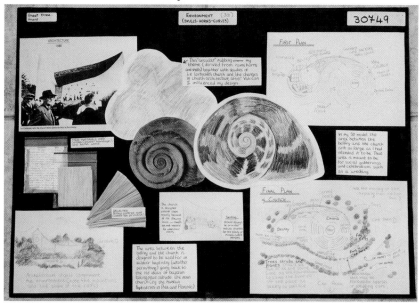

The circular motif is explored in the 3D preparation sheet. An architectural approach is also evident.

Fig. 5.24
***Support studies**.*

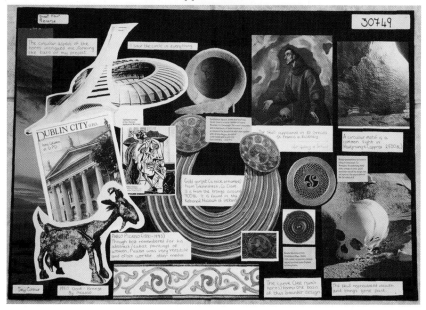

The circular shape is shown throughout the support studies, using historical material as well as magazine cut-outs and wallpaper borders. Explanations are given with each illustration.

THEME: WILDLIFE

Fig. 5.25
Completed painting.
For this painting the student made many drawings of a stuffed duck. The background was based on outdoor sketches. Note the obvious use of foreground, mid-ground and background to create an interesting painting and a feeling of depth.

Fig. 5.26
Completed batik.
A further development in the wildlife theme, using the same stuffed duck as a starting point. The natural resting habitat of the duck was studied for the background.

Fig. 5.27
Completed 3D in clay, with mixed media.
Using sketches and drawings, the student created this 3D model of the duck using clay, then painted it. The rest was constructed from straw, moss and twigs. The finished duck was approximately 20 cm high and 30 cm long.

THEME: NATURE

Fig. 5.28
Completed painting.
The starting point here was a stuffed fox which the student owned. The background, with this unusual winter sky, was derived from studies of nature in winter. The lively colour contrasts make the fox the focal point of this composition.

Fig. 5.29
Finished option: lino.
From many texture and linear studies, the fox's head emerged as a strong image for this print. The two lino prints show the effect of different-coloured backgrounds and a mixture of printing inks.

Fig. 5.30
Finished option: batik.
The fox dominates this piece of batik from the point of view of composition. The background provides a sense of depth as the colours fade into the distance.

THEME: ENTERTAINMENT/MUSIC

This student produced several finished pieces, which is not necessary. However, the pieces do illustrate different experiments in presentation and the overall effect is good. This sample shows a well-thought-out idea with variations in lettering.

Fig. 5.31
Graphic design: a video cover.

Fig. 5.32
Support studies.
The support studies show many graphic examples, including different types of lettering and composition.

THEME: ENTERTAINMENT/MUSIC

Fig. 5.33
Preparation for fabric printing.

Fig. 5.34
Finished fabric print.
This fabric print design is based on an eye motif. The eye is simplified and made suitable for a stencil. The design was worked into a half-drop repeat pattern. Two identical paper stencils were cut. Different dyes were used in an overlapping printing method.

THEME: RELAXING

Fig. 5.35
Preparation for painting.
Here we see five preliminary studies for the picture below. The contrast in drawing techniques is evident. Pencil, paint and pastel have been used.

Fig. 5.36
Finished painting (pastel).
This is an autumn scene taken directly from nature. The large leaves in the foreground emphasise the feeling of depth, leading the eye to the reader, who occupies a central position.

Fig. 5.37
Completed 3D.
The student worked directly from a model for this study of a reclining figure. It is made from clay and was later painted and glazed, using primary colours.

THEME: GROWTH AND DECAY

The idea behind this project was the life cycle of the butterfly, showing eggs, caterpillar, pupa, then butterfly.

Preparation for painting.

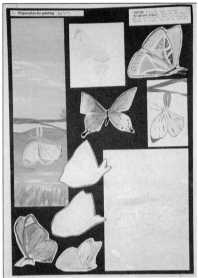

Fig. 5.38
This preparatory work includes landscape sketches and studies of the butterfly, executed in pencil, paint and coloured pencil.

Preparation for graphic design.

Fig. 5.40
Postage stamp, showing various studies, in paint and pastel, of the butterfly, floating on a rainbow of colour over a landscape.

Finished painting.

Fig. 5.39
Painting, showing butterflies in a summer landscape.

Finished graphic and design.

Fig. 5.41
Postage stamp.

THEME: GROWTH AND DECAY

Support studies for painting and graphic design.

Fig. 5.42

Finished 3D.

Fig. 5.43

Finished 3D.

Fig. 5.44

THEME: GROWTH AND DECAY

Preparatory sketches for option.

Fig. 5.45

Finished option: embroidery.

Fig. 5.46

Support studies for 3D and option.

Fig. 5.47

THEME: GROWING OLD

This project was developed from life drawing in the classroom.

Support studies for this project featured a study of artists' paintings of their mothers.

Preparation for painting.

Fig. 5.48
The preparatory sheet, which shows the three ages of women, was developed further in the painting.

Finished painting.

Fig. 5.49
The Three Ages of Women.

Finished graphic design.

Fig. 5.50
Book cover.

THEME: GROWING OLD

Preparation for option: batik.

Fig. 5.51

Preparation for 3D.

Fig. 5.52

Finished batik.

Fig. 5.53
A photograph of Pope John Paul II was used to develop drawings of the old woman in the batik.

Finished 3D.

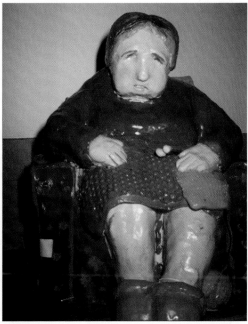

Fig. 5.54
Clay-modelled 3D of an old woman knitting.

THEME: IMAGINE

The starting point for this project was the Aboriginal Dreamtime.

Preparation for painting.

Fig. 5.55
Strange-looking trees were drawn, and painted studies of rock formations were made. Support studies of Australian paintings by Fred Williams helped to develop the rich colours in the painting.

Finished painting.

Fig. 5.56

Support studies for painting and graphic design.

Fig. 5.57
Support studies for the painting included the student's own photos of rock formations and examples of different artists' work. Examples of postage stamps and first-day covers were collected in support of the graphic design work.

THEME: IMAGINE

Finished postage stamp.

Fig. 5.58
For graphic design, a study of Australian rock paintings was made. A frog in X-ray style was developed in the preparatory work and an Art Nouveau style of lettering was developed to suit the image of the frog.

Finished 3D.

Fig. 5.59
Dreamtime mask, made from plaster, bandage, tree branches, coloured threads and Emu feathers.

Support studies for 3D and option.

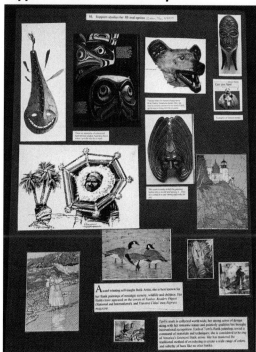

Fig. 5.60
Examples of masks from around the world were collected.

Finished option: batik.

Fig. 5.61
Dreamtime was again explored, as were examples of artists' batiks. The final piece shows a bird in flight against a sunset background.

THEME: THE ENTERTAINERS

This project features a study of the Ballets Russes, a ballet company which dazzled Europe in the early part of the twentieth century. It was famous for its spectacular costumes and sets, some of which were designed by well-known artists, including Picasso. These are shown in the support studies.

Preparatory drawing for batik.

Fig. 5.62
Pencil studies of dolls.

Finished batik.

Fig. 5.63

Finished painting.

Fig. 5.64
The preparatory work developed into this painting of a scene from the ballet Petrushka, *in which all the characters are dolls.*

THEME: THE ENTERTAINERS

Support studies for painting and graphic design.

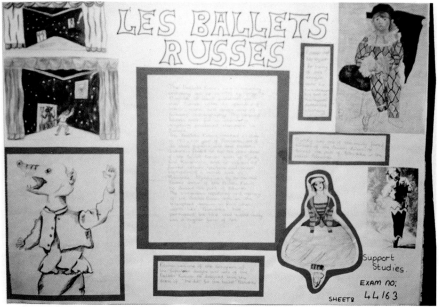

Fig. 5.65

Finished 3D.

Finished book cover.

Fig. 5.67
Pencil sketches of the student's own hands led to this graphic design, a cover for a book entitled Puppets.

Fig. 5.66
The 3D is a wire and papier maché doll of the main character, Petrushka, himself dressed in the costume worn by the famous dancer Nijinsky.

6. PAINTING

'Make a painting based on your starting point ... mixed media may be used.'

Preparatory studies

The first page of your examination paper states: 'Preparatory studies are an integral part of the project and must include the candidate's own observed/imagined images. Mere copying/tracing is not accepted.'

Preparatory studies for your painting must show investigation into your theme. If your preparatory sketches vary in size between A3 and A4, you will be able to present a few of them on your finished preparatory sheet. If you work on A2 size, you limit the amount of preparatory work you can show in your exam to one sheet. A few well-chosen sketches, some showing actual drawings from observation, and perhaps executed in different media, for example, pencil, pastel, ink, paint, etc., will not only add variety and interest to your work, but will help you choose your preferred media for your finished picture. Different media, like collage, mosaic, printing from found objects and rubbings, can broaden the scope of your preparatory studies and add an interesting approach to your work.

Size matters

Always remember to check the maximum size limit of your finished piece. All 2D work is limited to A2 size. It is recommended that you work about 2 cm smaller than A2 in both the height and width. This will leave a border when your work is mounted and will leave space for labelling your work. Remember, the finished product including the mount must not be more than A2 in size.

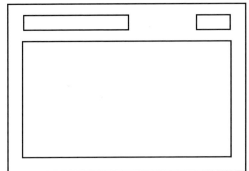

Fig. 6.1
Example of mounted 2D work. The space at the top is for your examination label and number.

Fig. 6.2
This preparatory study includes several pieces and demonstrates many approaches to painting. Pencil and paint have been used.

Fig. 6.3
This preparatory study shows just one approach (in pastel).

Most preparatory studies will involve drawing. One way of defining 'drawing' is: an image in which the main element is line. It is the quickest way of showing an object, idea or feeling in a pictorial way. Drawings differ depending on the materials used. Pencil drawings have a totally different character to pastel or paint. Your preparatory drawings may be called sketches.

Suitable materials for drawing are pencil, charcoal, pastel crayons, chalks, felt-tip markers, inks, etc. Each drawing material has a character of its own. Many people prefer to use two or three drawing materials at most. Use whatever medium you are comfortable and happy with. If using pencil, make sure that you have two different grades of softness to work with, for example, a 2B and a 4B, as this combination will give a great variety of tones, add interest and depth to your work and give it a 3D quality.

Tonal scale

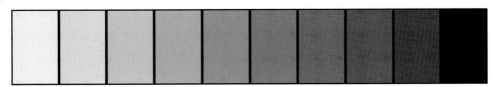

Fig. 6.4

Drawing techniques

When you wish to achieve a tonal effect in your work, some of the following techniques may be useful: blending and smudging, cross-hatching, scribble-hatching, pointillism or planes.

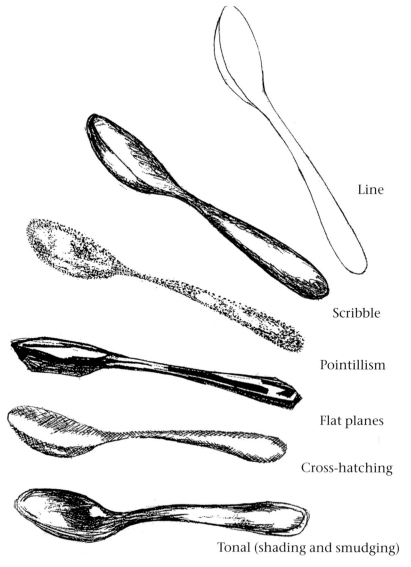

Line

Scribble

Pointillism

Flat planes

Cross-hatching

Tonal (shading and smudging)

Fig. 6.5
Different techniques and approaches to drawing.

Your preparatory sketches may include detailed studies that may form part of the finished painting. If the subject of your picture is based on natural and/or man-made objects, then detailed studies may be made of the shapes and proportions of the objects and the colour and patterns found on them.

Light source

Other considerations with regard to your picture are:

- time of day – this is shown by the direction of the dominant light (remember that light can have a natural or artificial source)
- the season
- the weather conditions.

Which format?

Your picture can have either a vertical or horizontal format. Vertical pictures give a sense of activity while horizontal pictures can create a sense of peace and calm.

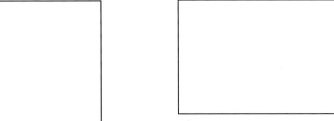

Fig. 6.6
Left: Vertical/portrait.
Above: Horizontal/landscape.

Fig. 6.7
Theme – Relaxing. Sheet 1 – preparation for painting.
Starting point: a seated figure reading a book (horizontal format).

Arrangement/composition

If your picture involves a landscape, townscape or seascape, then you may wish to consider the background, mid-ground and foreground sections of your picture when making your preparatory sketches.

| Background |
| Mid-ground |
| Foreground |

Fig. 6.8

In the foreground we tend to find the larger objects, and sometimes these objects project backwards into the mid-ground and even the background. An example of this would be a tree. We can see objects in the foreground more clearly because they are close to us, and so, in this style of picture, the lightest lights and the darkest darks will always be in the foreground.

Objects get smaller and lighter in colour as they move into the distance. This is called atmospheric perspective. In the mid-ground we may find streets, roads, groups of houses, fields and forests, etc.

The pictures in Fig. 6.9 and Fig. 6.10 are examples of one-point perspective. Both pictures are dominated by the mid-ground and background. However, if, say, a person, a broken fence or a gate was added in the foreground, this would create a focal point and attention would be drawn away from the mid-ground and background.

Fig. 6.9

Fig. 6.10
A twist in the road gives a greater feeling of depth.

Examples of arrangement/composition

Sky and mountains are always in the background. Sometimes the background forms more than two-thirds of a picture. A good example of this is the painting called *Mares and Foals in a River Landscape* by George Stubbs (Fig. 6.11). In this painting the mares and the tree occupy a large section of the foreground. The mid-ground occupies a very small area, yet it conveys tremendous distance, while the clouds in the background further enhance this sense of distance.

$\frac{2}{3}$

$\frac{1}{3}$

Fig. 6.11
Mares and Foals in a River Landscape *by George Stubbs (1724–1806).*

Fig. 6.12
La Madeleine a La Veilleuse *(1635)*
by Georges de la Tour. La Madeleine
*uses an artificial light source contained
within the picture. The contrast of
strong light and dark shadows gives
this painting a sense of drama.*

Fig. 6.13
The Magpie *by Claude Monet (1840–1926)*
*shows us an interesting observation of natural
light, with the blue shadows coming towards us.
We are also aware of the season – winter – and
the weather conditions – snow.*

Plan your picture to be engaging and interesting. The viewer's eye should be led into the picture by the composition (see pages 82 and 83).

Composition therefore involves arranging things in a pleasing and balanced way. Any picture or any surface design, whether realistic or abstract, should use the guidelines of composition to its advantage. The aim is to keep the viewer's attention, leading their eye in and around the work/picture.

Where should the focal point be?

Composition can be much more difficult to define when applied to abstract pictures or designs. Perhaps it is best to consider avoiding these unless you have a lot of experience.

One rule is to avoid having the focal point smack in the middle of your picture. This can lead to very monotonous work. Keep larger objects in the foreground balanced by smaller objects further away.

Fig. 6.14

Fig. 6.15
The arrows show the direction your eye takes in the picture in Fig. 6.14.

Fig. 6.16
This is an example of a composition that leads your eyes in and around the picture, with the trees acting as barriers keeping your eye focused towards the centre. The road leads your eye towards the cottage, while the clouds bring your eye down to the mountains and the mountains keep your eye low in the picture. The people in the foreground going towards the house reinforce the stable composition. The light source adds a 3D effect, whereas showing the sun might have destroyed the atmosphere.

Remember that your plans and sketches must be kept safely for further reference. They show the development of ideas that lead you to your final image.

Perspective

As you are working on the composition, check your perspective.

One-point perspective

If you draw a railway track or straight road – like the one in Fig. 6.17 – you will notice that the sides of the road seem to meet in the distance, even though we know that in reality they are parallel lines. The place at which the lines seem to meet is called the vanishing point. Vanishing points are often on the horizon, but you can also have vanishing points above and below the horizon line. The position of the horizon in your picture depends on your eye level. The illustrations in Figs 6.17–19 show different eye levels.

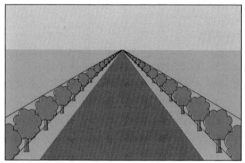

Fig. 6.17
Bird's eye view – from the air.

Fig. 6.18
Normal view – from human eye level (standing).

Fig. 6.19
Worm's eye view – from ground level.

Colours also change as they go out of view, or as they recede into the distance. Most will appear to fade because of the weather conditions and the earth's atmosphere.

Styles of painting

Painting is the application of some type of colouring material onto a flat surface. Paintings can be realistic, semi-realistic or abstract.

- Realistic means showing the real work in a photographic style. It is recognisaable, like impressionism and pointillism.

- Semi-realistic painting uses styles such as pointillism or that of the Impressionists to convey images.

- Abstract art is non-realistic art where colour, line, pattern, shape and tone are more important than the subject itself. It is non-representational. Mondrian made abstract paintings.

Fig. 6.20
Still Life *by Pieter Claesz, an example of* ***realistic*** *painting.*

Fig. 6.21
Composition (*1929*), by Piet Mondrian (*1872–1944*), *is an example of* ***abstract*** *painting. Mondrian used straight black lines and shapes of primary colours to form this work. His aim was for perfect compositional balance. Mondrian was a leading member of De Stijl movement.*

Fig. 6.22
Wheat Fields with Sheaves *by* **Vincent van Gogh**. *An example of* ***semi-realistic*** *painting.*

7. GRAPHIC DESIGN

Graphic design deals with the more functional side of art. Nearly all graphic design contains some form of lettering and/or image.

Graphic design is just about everywhere. It is part of everyday life and it is virtually impossible to avoid it. From the time you reach out for that packet of cereal in the morning to the time you come home at night and switch on the TV, you will have encountered hundreds of graphic designs without even realising it.

Graphic design can be found on packets, tins, jars, labels, leaflets, catalogues, brochures, cassettes tapes, CD covers, letterheads, envelopes, stamps, newspapers, magazines, books, tickets, programmes, posters, billboards, buses, trains, timetables, logos, signs, bags, cheques, credit cards, telephone cards, shopfronts, banners and T-shirts. Apart from T-shirts, none of these items could function without some sort of graphic design.

Fig. 7.1

Ordinary Level or Higher Level

Remember:

- If you are doing the *Ordinary Level* paper, you have a choice between painting and graphic design.
- If you are doing the *Higher Level* paper, you must do both sections.

Which graphic design shall I choose?

There is a wide choice in the graphic design section. You are required to design and make *one* of the following in your exam project:

- poster
- video cover
- book jacket
- postage stamp
- record sleeve
- CD cover
- logo
- brochure.

What you choose to work on may be determined by what you have been doing in class. It is often advisable to do something that has been tried and tested.

Still not sure?

Look around for examples of each category with your own theme in mind. Don't always pick what you think may be the easiest choice. Pick what will show off your particular skills. Remember, the design process must be gone through, no matter what your choice may be.

What to do first

Collect all sorts of graphic designs, preferably examples that relate to your theme. These will be your support studies examples; they won't all necessarily relate directly to your theme, but may help you later with lettering or give you ideas on how to develop your images. Make sure to give reasons for the items you finally select as support studies, for example, what attracted you to it and how you found it useful.

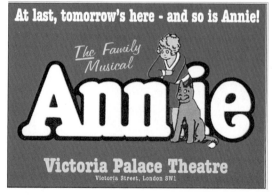

Fig. 7.2
This style of lettering is attractive and clear.

Rough sketches and experiments

Before making a decision on what to do for your final graphic design, it is advisable to try out ideas in the different categories briefly beforehand. All attempts in the form of rough sketches and experiments may go on your preparation sheet, so nothing will be lost.

Lettering

Fig. 7.3
A simple block alphabet. A basic knowledge of lettering is essential. This is strong 'no nonsense' block lettering, which is suitable for most graphic designs. It can be developed in many ways to add interest and style to your work.

Measurements – recommended sizes

The maximum size of the graphic design is A2 (59 cm x 42 cm). It is advisable to work smaller than this in order to allow space for labelling. Otherwise the labels will have to be put over your design and will spoil the finished piece.

Fig. 7.4
Poster (54 cm x 36 cm). Work upright/vertical and at less than full size. Vertical is preferable to horizontal.

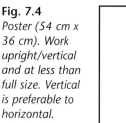

Fig. 7.5
Video cover (spine = 19.5/20 cm x 3 cm; back and front = 19.5/20 cm x 11.5/12 cm). Work actual size or larger to scale.

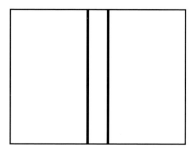

Fig. 7.6
Book jacket (20.5 cm x (8 + 13 + 2.5 + 13 + 8) cm. Work actual size.

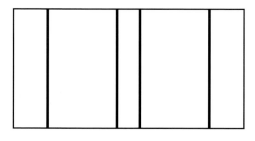

Fig. 7.7
Postage stamp (19 cm x 27.5 cm, including the perforations, which are about 5 mm deep – a little less than A4 overall). Work larger. Reduce the finished design to actual postage-stamp size of 3 cm x 4 cm for presentation with your full-size finished piece.

Fig. 7.8
Record sleeve (a square, 31 cm x 31 cm). Work actual size.

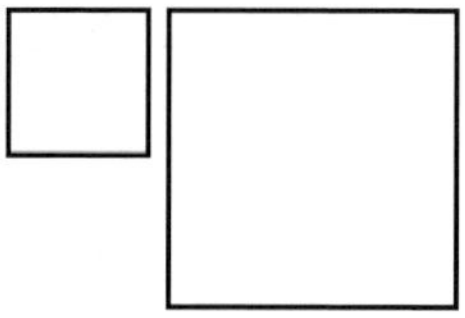

Fig. 7.9
Logo (minimum 10 cm x 10 cm; maximum 20 cm x 20 cm or a measured rectangle).

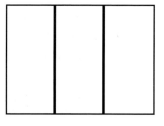

Fig. 7.10
CD cover (almost a square, 12 cm x 11.75 cm with a 1.23 cm edge). Work larger to scale.

Fig. 7.11
Brochure A4 (21 cm x 29.5 cm divided into three parts).

Posters

Function: to convey a specific message.

A poster should attract attention and retain it for a brief but intense moment, long enough to motivate or provoke its audience. It can make the viewer laugh, reflect, question, protest, absorb, recoil or react in some way. The poster should be clear and simple and easy to read. It should succeed in conveying its message.

Different types of poster:

- a general message poster (including propaganda)
- an event poster
- advertising (selling a product).

Before you start designing a poster, decide what type of poster it is, otherwise you will not have a clear focus, your message will not be clear and your poster will lose its impact.

Fig. 7.12
Three Dog Night poster.

Event posters checklist:

1. What is the event?
2. Where is the event?
3. What date is the event taking place?
4. What time is the event taking place?
5. What is the admission fee (if any)?

Remember, posters are generally viewed from a distance, so be careful not to include too much detail.

Practical guide for designing a poster

Fig. 7.13
First draw up your measurements: 54 cm x 36 cm, then draw a margin of 2 cm or 3 cm to prevent you from taking your lettering right up to the edge.

Fig. 7.19
Note how the car in this Junior Cert student's work is almost coming out at the viewer.

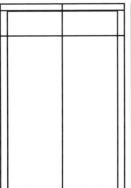 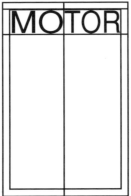

Fig. 7.14
Next draw a line down the centre – this will help you if you are doing a symmetrical poster.

Fig. 7.15
Two-line guide.

Fig. 7.16
Three-line guide.

Take care over your lettering. Some letters like 'M' are wider than the rest and will push your letters over a little. You should always draw two guidelines, as they will keep your lettering straight, and sometimes you will need three lines, depending on the style of lettering, its positioning and shape. See the examples on the left.

Fig. 7.18

Fig. 7.17

It is probably better to put the image in first, as the lettering can be worked around it, through it or above it. Try different approaches, different images, vary the layout, etc.

Approach

Never go straight into a design. All your attempts at various approaches and images should be kept safely and used on your preparation sheet. Note all difficulties, together with how you managed to solve any problems.

It is better to work calmly and consistently than to rush into your project, making needless mistakes. However, you must work continuously and deliberately; this is not a time to relax, especially if you have left things rather late.

Measure the lettering/words and design for your poster and create balance between them. If you can think of something catchy using just a few words, use that. For example, 'breaking all barriers' in the Motor Show poster in Fig. 7.19 is very effective.

Colours

When it comes to colour, choose striking colours. You could use contrasting colours, such as blue and orange – they shout at each other! – very good for attracting attention to the poster. Limit the number of colours you use – too many will detract from your message. Use paint (if possible), as it is more effective and striking. Coloured pencils need a lot of work to be effective, though some of the water-soluble coloured pencils can give quite good results. When doing your lettering, ideally use a marker or a felt-tip pen, as long as this suits the lettering. Use a ruler to have more control of the edges. Brushes can be a bit awkward, unless you are very skilful with them. Again, try out what suits you best: *don't leave anything to chance.*

Remember that all of your experiments and sketches can be used on your preparation sheet!

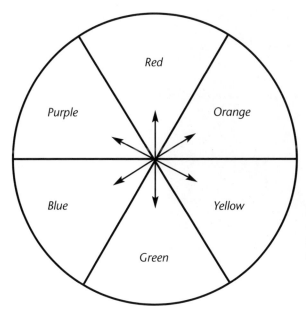

Fig. 7.20
Colour wheel showing the complementary pairs of colours.

Creative lettering

In graphic design, lettering and image go hand in hand. A good combination of lettering and image makes for a more informative and interesting end product.

The eye-catching posters on these two pages illustrate different themes (entertainment, outer space, drugs and war). Note the different types of lettering used and how they fit with each poster's theme.

Fig. 7.21
Saturday Night Fever
poster/brochure. When words form the image and the image in turn forms the words, the result can be dramatic and very striking.

Fig. 7.22
The Red Hat Restaurant *by Wes Wilson. Clear, simple and imaginative – the ingredients for a good poster, brochure or any graphic design.*

Fig. 7.23
By Anne C. Patterson.

Fig. 7.25
Irish anti-drugs poster.

Fig. 7.24
By Schulz-Neudamm. Dramatised by its length.

Fig. 7.26
By Paul Nash, 1918.

Video covers

If you choose this category, you can work your design to the actual size, or scale it accordingly – but go larger if anything, *not* smaller.

Fig. 7.27
Recommended measurements.

11.5/12 cm   3 cm   11.5/12 cm

19.5/20 cm

Video covers generally include:

- a title (with suitable lettering)
- an image (attractive, simple)
- actors or stars
- film grading (for example, 'U', 'PG', '15', '18')
- information about the video
- the production company's name and/or logo
- the production company's website address
- a bar code.

Layout = front, back and spine.

For the information text, use newsprint upside-down, as you are not expected to compose a story or write text as part of the project – just indicate it in the layout.

The spine should give all the essential information about the video, for example, the title, grading and company logo, because videos are usually stacked like books on a shelf. Pay attention to spacing, measurements and proportions in your layout; video covers have a similar function to posters in that they must attract attention and their message must be clear, although they are viewed more closely and can therefore include more detail.

Do not forget to research video covers generally to give you lots of ideas and information towards your support studies.

Book jackets

The layout for book jackets is similar to video covers except for the additional flaps which give more information about the book.

| 8 cm | 13 cm | 2.5 cm | 13 cm | 8 cm |

Fig. 7.28
Recommended measurements.

Book jackets generally include:

- a title
- an image
- an author
- information about the book
- the publisher's name or logo
- the publisher's website address
- a bar code
- the ISBN number.

Layout = front, back, spine and two flaps.

As with video covers, use newsprint upside-down to indicate the information text in the layout, as you are not expected to compose a story or write text.

Leaving space around the edges of your design will improve your layout and you can cut out a small photo of the author from a magazine to put on the left flap.

Remember: Researching and collecting examples of book jackets will help you with ideas for the layout.

Postage stamps

To some, the postage stamp project may seem to be the easiest category in graphic design, but because of this, the layout and impact of the finished piece of work must be exemplary.

Recommended measurements: 19 cm x 27.5 cm, including the perforations which are 5 mm deep – overall a little less than A4 in size. Stamps may be horizontal or vertical.

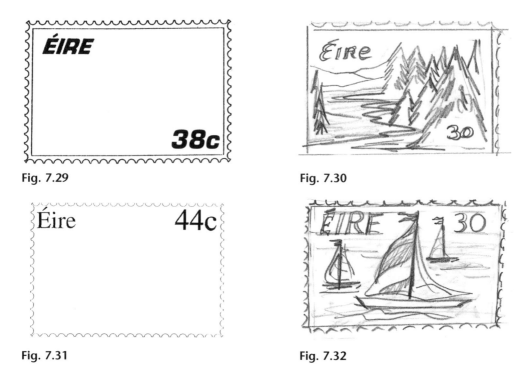

Fig. 7.29   Fig. 7.30

Fig. 7.31   Fig. 7.32

The positioning of the country of origin and the price are very important, as these details should be clear and easy to read and the background should not detract from them.

All stamps must include:

- the country of origin (the head of the monarch in the case of the UK)
- the price.

For full appreciation of your stamp design, reduce it in the preparatory stages in order to see its potential impact as a 'real' stamp.

Stamps are easy to collect and so support studies should pose no problem. Commemorative stamps are difficult to design, as they often have to show something, like a building, that does not reduce well.

Record sleeves/CD covers

As record sleeves and CD covers are so similar (apart from scale), they will be dealt with together. They are basically square in shape, but watch the final measurements – the CD cover is slightly wider (horizontal) than it is long (vertical). Recording companies generally use the same design on both, though records are fast going out of production because of the popularity of CDs.

All record sleeves and CD covers should have:

- a title
- an artist (performer, band/group, orchestra, singer)
- an image (this could be the artist or the title or some other image)
- music/song list (this could be tied in with the title and the artist)
- or a combination of all or some of the above.

Fig. 7.33
Title = Made in Heaven; Artist = Queen; Image = Freddy Mercury and scenery.

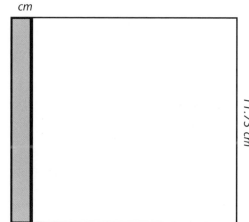

1.23 cm

11.75 cm

12 cm

Fig. 7.34
Recommended measurements

Recommended measurements: Record sleeve – 31 cm x 31 cm (see Fig. 7.34 for CD cover measurements).

Layout = front cover; or, as an alternative option, the front *and* back covers.

Record sleeves and CD covers often act as 'image makers' for a group or artist; special lettering and/or colours have often been associated with certain artists.

Logos

A logo is a trademark image or emblem by which a business or institution can be recognised at a glance.

Strictly speaking, logos do not use letters or words but portray a symbolic image. However, logotypes usually use letters alone or combine letters with symbolic images. The term 'logos' is used quite loosely and includes reference to both logos and logotypes.

Logos are usually kept simple in order to make a quick visual impact, but to produce a good logo you might need to make many drawings and do a lot of research to come up with an eye-catching and memorable design. Colours should be kept to a minimum to get maximum impact.

Logos come in all shapes and sizes; however, as a guide, perhaps your finished work should be a square, between 10 cm x 10 cm and 20 cm x 20 cm or a rectangle, for example, 10 cm x 20 cm, and the image you develop should be sharp, clear and self-explanatory.

Fig. 7.35
Examples of logos and logotypes.

Brochures

Function: to advertise.

As brochures are viewed close up, you can afford to have a lot more detail in this than, say, on a poster. The front of a brochure has similar qualities to a book jacket.

Fig. 7.36

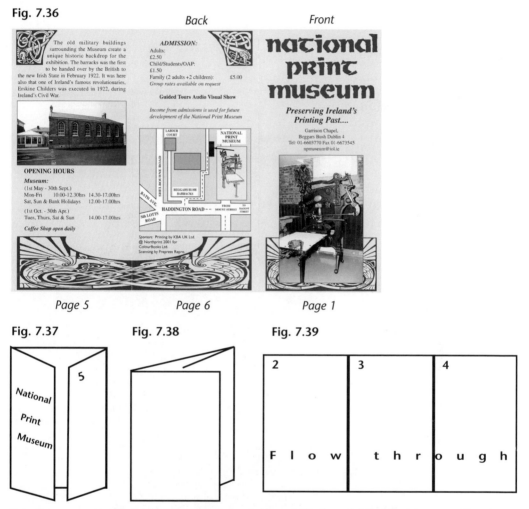

Back   Front

Page 5   Page 6   Page 1

Fig. 7.37   **Fig. 7.38**   **Fig. 7.39**

Brochures are usually folded into three parts, so an A4 sheet folded in this way will make the six 'pages' of your brochure.

The design for a brochure should be consistent and provide a sense of unity throughout. The background colour or design, lettering layout, pictures and illustrations should provide visual interest and, of course, all the necessary information.

Note to save time
Cut-out newsprint turned upside down may be used to indicate text areas.

8. 3D

The 3D part of the paper is divided into three sections:

- modelling
- carving
- construction.

You only have to carry out *one* of the above.

Choose one you are familiar with. Modelling and construction tend to be more popular than carving, as they deal with positives (building or adding to) rather than negatives (taking away). Still, it is a good idea to have tried out each different type of work before committing yourself to one alone.

Modelling – clay

Clay is very suitable for modelling. Though all clays can be used, it is advisable to use a heavy grog clay or synthetic clay, as these kinds can be worked a lot before drying out. Work with wooden tools (the type used in pottery – see page 109).

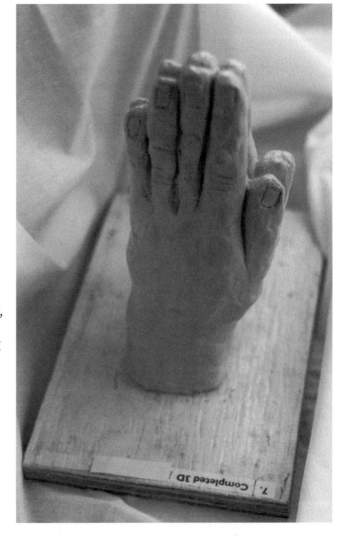

Fig. 8.1
Praying or joined hands. *A 3D model executed in clay.*

Notes of warning:

- Avoid too many jutting out or extended points, as they tend to get damaged easily.
- Don't get tied up in details until the main shape or form is worked out.

Fig. 8.2
The Horseman *by Marino Marini. If you choose an animal theme, you will need to construct a wire or wooden armature as a support frame.*

Fig. 8.3
Plaques may look simple, but because they concentrate on only one side, they are challenging to model. This form of modelling is called 'relief'.

Fig. 8.4
Texture can play an important role in modelling, adding interest to your piece.

Modelling – other materials

■ Plasticine – usually only used for small pieces, for example, in animation.

■ Papier maché – a mixture of wallpaper paste (see packet for mixing instructions) or PVA glue and paper. It is ideal for larger pieces of work and very popular for making masks for festivals, as it dries to a very light weight. It can be used on its own, but is more versatile when built around some form of support such as wire mesh, a balloon or even a lightbulb. Only the wire remains as a support, as balloons are burst and lightbulbs discarded when the papier maché is dry.

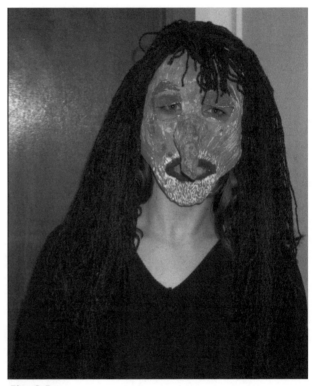

Fig. 8.5
Mask made from papier maché.

■ Plaster – very versatile for modelling, especially when using gypsona (bandage, pre-soaked with plaster), which only needs to be dipped in water to make it malleable.

■ Wax – for example, wax models in a wax museum – can be expensive, difficult to obtain and time-consuming to use.

Fig. 8.6
Boot made from papier maché.

Carving

Carving is all about taking away material from a main block *en masse*. To do this successfully it is necessary to plan your work carefully.

Carvers often build up a material in order to cut or carve into it, like the students from Tokyo who carved *Hell of the Rush Hour* from sand – see Fig. 8.7.

Fig. 8.7
Hell of the Rush Hour.

Plaster

For the purposes of the exam, plaster is probably the best material to use for carving. First, make a block of plaster. All you need is plaster, water and a wax- or plastic-coated container (the type used for milk or orange juice). When the plaster has set, just peel or cut away the container. Steel implements like chisels and files can be used to carve the plaster and sandpaper can be used for fine finishes.

Soap can also be used for carving, though the pieces available tend to be relatively small and it can therefore be rather limiting.

Fig. 8.8

Construction

Almost any material is suitable for 3D construction work. A mixture of found objects can be stuck together and a variety of materials can be carved, cut or twisted (bottle caps, paperclips, cloth – the list is endless).

Fig. 8.9
*It is often said that **Edgar Degas** was the first to use mixed media with his **Little Dancer Aged Fourteen (1880)**, which uses bronze, muslin and silk.*

Fig. 8.10
*Construction can lead to all sorts of imaginery fantasies, like **Tom Horn's Installation** mobiles. Moving 3D work has found its place in the art world and has become very popular in recent decades.*

EXAMPLES OF STUDENTS' 3D WORK

Fig. 8.11
Theme – Nature. Modelled from clay.

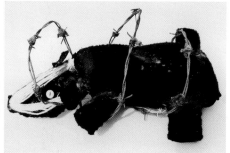

Fig. 8.12
Theme – Nature. Construction in mixed media.

Fig. 8.13
Theme – Music. Construction using wood, card and pipe cleaners.

Fig. 8.14
Theme – Woodcutter. Construction in wood and wire.

Fig. 8.15
Theme – Dancing. Modelled from clay.

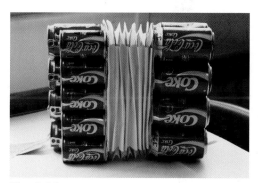

Fig. 8.16
Theme – Music/My hobby. Construction in cans and card.

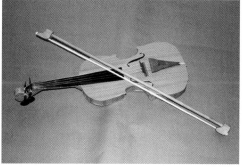

Fig. 8.17
Theme – Irish music. Mixed-media construction in card, contact, wood.

9. OPTIONS (CRAFT)

Pottery/ceramics

Pottery may be used for 3D or as an option (craft). Pottery is made from specially mixed clay. It can be formed into many different shapes using different approaches and techniques.

Fig. 9.1
Nicholas Mosse *is a studio potter in Co. Kilkenny. He uses motifs which are drawn from traditional Irish images.*

Traditionally, pottery refers to pots, plates and vases. However, this narrow view is only one aspect of pottery, which can include most objects made out of clay using the different techniques associated with pottery.

Pottery as an exam option

Before starting on your pottery project, first make a brainstorming list. Then make sketches and studies based on your theme. At this point your theme will have progressed and expanded in a number of ways and you should have collected plenty of support studies. Find the ones that directly relate to pottery. Postcards of artists' work in pottery are available throughout the country.

Materials needed for pottery

You will need:

- clay – there are many different types, depending on what you wish to make and what technique you wish to use
- a kiln to fire your finished piece
- glazes and slips
- a potter's wheel.

However, a kiln, glazes and a wheel are only necessary if you wish to pursue pottery more seriously.

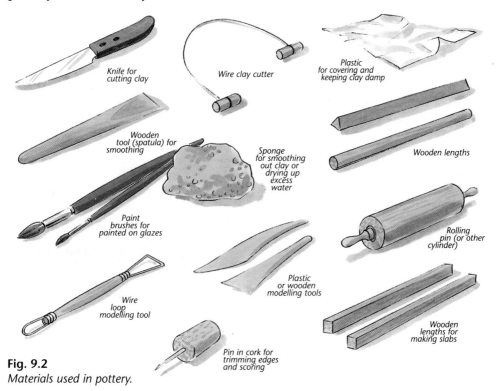

Fig. 9.2
Materials used in pottery.

Schools that intend to teach pottery should provide the following equipment:

- solid benches
- kiln furniture (shelves, shelf props)
- clay stores (bins with lids)
- a kiln (with thermostat)
- drying-out shelves
- shelves or storage space for biscuit pottery awaiting gloss/glaze firing
- pug mill.

Each student should have access to the following tools:

- special pottery or modelling wooden and plastic tools – in all shapes, either bought or made
- cutting wire – twisted wire attached to a small wooden stick as a handle
- a wire loop tool
- a point-ended knife
- a corked needle (for trimming)
- a rolling pin or round length of wood.

Other tools may be created from wood, discarded pieces of plastic, old pens, etc.

How to make pottery

First you must choose what technique you wish to use. If you choose to do hand-built pottery, you have a further choice between:

- a pinch or thumb pot
- a coil pot
- a slab pot.

Note: Clay shrinks as it dries, so always work a little larger to allow for this.

The pinch pot or thumb pot

This is one of the easiest techniques. You simply roll some clay into a ball, then push your thumb into the middle and work your way around it, bringing up the sides. When finished the pot may be left plain, or you can decorate it with indented marks forming a pattern, or paint on a glaze afterwards.

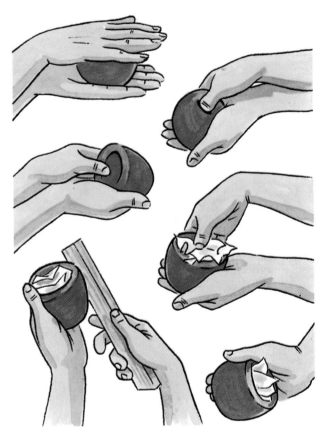

Fig. 9.3
Making a thumb pot.

The coil pot

This technique consists of rolling out long worm-like lengths and coiling them on top of each other on a clay base. The length of the pieces depend on the size of the pot you wish to construct. Though the lengths coiled together look good, it is advisable to work them into each other to bond them.

If the coils are not sealed (scored on the back with a modelling tool), they will split and break at any weak point. Decoration may be added later using more coils, by making indentations or by glazing it later.

Slab pots

After wedging (getting the air out of the clay) you must roll out your clay, or cut it into flat slabs. The slabs should then be left to dry until they are 'leather hard' (not fully dry or they will break up when you start to work them). Planning beforehand is essential, as the wrong calculation could ruin all your work (this applies to anything you undertake). The edges can be joined by scoring, that is, roughening the edges with a fork-like tool before pasting it together with soft clay or slip. Work the edges together carefully and smooth off the surface with a sponge. Slab pots tend to be geometrical shapes because of the technique used to make them.

Fig. 9.4
Making a coil pot.

Fig. 9.5
Making a slab pot.

Wheel pottery and moulded pottery

Wheel pottery
Unless you have a pottery wheel available *and* have plenty of time to practise, this technique is not recommended. You must learn how to centre the clay (called 'throwing') before you start to 'pull up' a pot. Clay must be kept moist and the thickness of the pot must be even.

Moulded pottery
This is relatively easy. You can take a mould from many things provided you use a barrier (like slip or Vaseline) to prevent your clay from sticking. Plaster is recommended as you can make your own mould and with the slab technique (explained under 'Slab pots', page 111) make your own piece of work.

Fig. 9.6
Moulded pottery.

Finishing off your pottery piece

The best way to finish off any pottery piece is to fire it in a kiln. Pottery normally needs two firings. The first one makes the clay solid, but it is still porous (that is, not waterproof) – this is called the 'biscuit firing'. The second firing is done after a glaze is applied, and this is called the 'glaze firing', which leaves the pottery piece waterproof. However, if waterproofing your pottery is not necessary, you can paint or polish it after the biscuit firing using paint and a varnish or liquid shoe polish (suitable for masks, etc.).

EXAMPLES OF POTTERY

Fig. 9.8
Cut-out/slab pot.
Suitable for wood.

Fig. 9.7
*This pottery owl was made from a mould designed by the artist **Oisin Kelly**. A suitable type of work for birds or flight themes.*

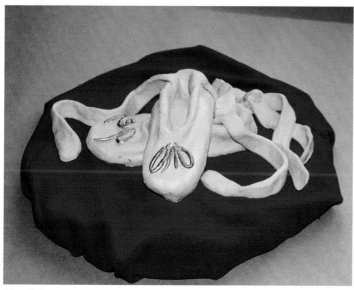

Fig. 9.9
Pottery shoes, painted finish. Suitable for dance or shoe themes.

Batik

A batik is created by drawing an image with hot wax onto fabric. The fabric is then immersed into a dye bath. The wax will resist the dye and the part covered with wax will hold the original fabric colour. For this reason, light-coloured fabric is most suitable.

Batik itself is a very old craft that originated in Indonesia (an island in South-East Asia). The word *batik* is Javanese and means writing in wax. It is a very popular medium and is used by many artists throughout the world.

Batik as an exam option

Before starting your batik, you should make a brainstorming list. Then make sketches and studies based on your theme. At this point your theme will have progressed and expanded in a number of ways and you should have collected plenty of support studies. Find the ones that relate directly to batik. Postcards of artists' work in batik are available in craft shops throughout the country.

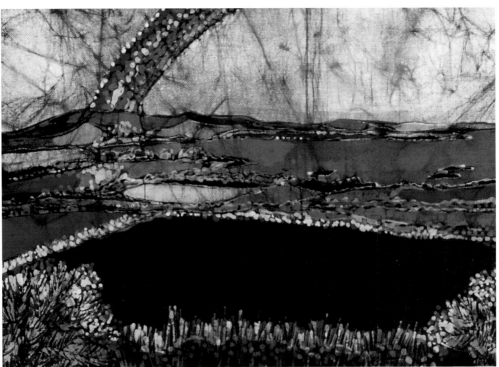

Fig. 9.10
Rainbow over Baltimore, Co. Cork. *From a batik on linen by* ***Bernadette Madden.***

Fig. 9.11
Christmas in St Patrick's Cathedral, Dublin. *From a batik by* ***Bernadette Madden.*** *Suitable for themes like churches, architecture and buildings.*

Fig. 9.12
From **Thatched House near Ardmore,** *a batik by Bernadette Madden.* *Note the use of linear strokes to form the texture of the thatched house, and the pattern at the ridge running underneath the chimney. The crackles in the wax add a nice sense of texture to the sky.*

Designing for batik

When creating a design for batik you must consider how you want your finished batik to look. There are two ways of dying a batik: one is to use a dye bath for each colour, and the second is to paint or sponge on the dyes. Both give very different results, so it is important to keep this in mind at the design stage.

Method one

With this method the fabric is waxed, then immersed in a bath of cold dye. It is important to use cold dye, otherwise the wax will melt. If a number of colours are to be used in your batik, the first colour should be the lightest, as the remainder of the colours will go on top of this. Allow the dyed fabric to dry, then wax the areas of the fabric that are to remain the first colour, and dye again. By using the lightest colours first and adding progressively darker colours, the finished work will always look harmonious. Fig. 9.13 is a good example of this technique.

Fig. 9.13
This is an example of a student's batik using method one. The theme of this project was 'pets'.

Dye 1 = yellow

Dye 2 =   } orange/red

Dye 3 = red   } mid-blue   } mid-brown } deep brown

Dye 4 =   } deep grey

Method two

In this method the fabric is waxed in a similar manner to method one, but because areas can be isolated from each other, this allows each area to have its own group of harmonious colours which are applied with a brush or sponge, resulting in a very colourful finished piece. See Fig. 9.14.

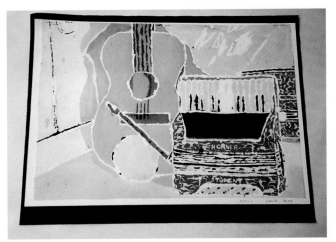

Fig. 9.14
Method two was used in this batik on the theme of 'My hobby'.

Area 1 – sky:
a. **Wax in cloudy areas, dye with light blue.**
b. **Wax in some light blue area and dye with mid-blue.**

Area 2 – mid-ground:
a. **Dye with light green for distant hills.**
b. **Wax in background hills and the outline of some fields.**
c. **Dye with mid-green.**
d. **Wax mid-green areas, perhaps using a variety of textural strokes.**
e. **Dye perhaps an olive green.**

Fig. 9.15
Example of method two: a landscape scene, initially divided into four areas. Each area is outlined in wax.

Area 3 – foreground:
This might be a lake area and so might be worked in a similar way to the sky.

Area 4 – tree:
This area can be waxed and dyed several times, perhaps using a variety of tans and browns.

Materials needed for batik

You will need:

- fine- to medium-weight white fabric – cotton is the most suitable
- wax pot (thermostatically controlled) and batik wax
- brushes or *tjantings* for applying the wax to the fabric
- suitable fabric dyes
- a wooden frame and drawing pins for stretching your fabric
- old newspapers
- buckets for mixing the dye baths
- an iron and clean newsprint for ironing out the wax.

When you have assembled all of the equipment necessary:

1. Draw your image onto your fabric, using a pencil.
2. Stretch the fabric onto the frame using drawing pins.
3. Cover with wax the parts of your fabric that you wish to remain white using a brush or *tjanting*.
4. Either paint or sponge the dye on or immerse in dye, depending on whether you are following method one or method two.

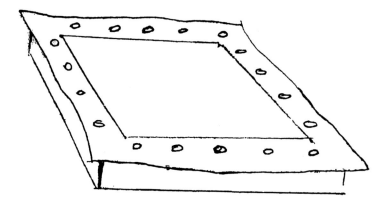

Fig. 9.16
Frame with fabric stretched onto it.

Batik is a relatively simple craft, but you need to take care when using the hot wax.

EXAMPLES OF STUDENTS' BATIKS

Fig. 9.17
On the theme of buildings and
their occupants.

Fig. 9.18
On the
theme of
music.

Fig. 9.19
On the
theme of
water.

Fig. 9.20
On the theme of water.

Screen printing

A screen print is created when printing ink is forced through a mesh that has a stencil attached to it. The cut-away parts of the stencil allow the ink to pass through to form the printed surface. The advantage of using a stencil is that you can reproduce the same image many times. A screen print can be produced in one or more colours.

Fig. 9.21
A stencil of a flower shape.

Fig. 9.22
A simple print of a flower shape.

Designing for screen printing

Develop your theme and make a study of it in a few flat colours. Choose one colour (let's say blue) and draw onto your stencil paper the outline of only those shapes containing blue. If you are hoping to achieve a third colour, for example, green, by overprinting yellow on blue, then you will need to draw out the green shapes also. Place your stencil paper on a board and cut out the designated areas. Securely attach your stencil to the printing screen. Place the screen on top of a sheet of paper that has already been registered (precisely lined up) on a base board. Register your screen. Pour ink onto it and, using a squeegee, pull the ink across the screen. Lift the screen and you will see the printed image on your sheet of paper.

When developing a design for screen print, try to contrast line and texture with larger open areas. Fine delicate lines are best avoided. They are difficult to cut and prone to clogging up with ink when printing.

Materials needed for screen printing

You will need:

- a screen
- a squeegee
- stencil paper or film
- a cutting knife
- a board
- printing inks
- masking tape
- paper.

Fig. 9.23
Theme – Water: waste not, want not. This three-colour screen print was made using paper stencils.

EXAMPLES OF STUDENTS' SCREEN PRINTS

Fig. 9.24
Theme – Water: waste not, want not. This three-colour screen print was made using two paper stencils. Two colours, purple and yellow, were used. A third colour, brown, was achieved by overprinting yellow and purple.

Fig. 9.25
Theme – Pets. This is a four-colour screen print. A fifth colour has been achieved by overprinting.

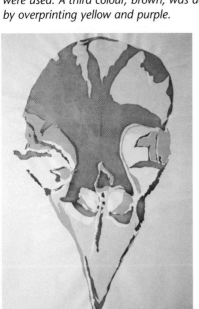

Fig. 9.26
Theme – My hobby: birdwatching. This three-colour screen print of a skull led to the study of the skeletons of birds.

Fig. 9.27
Theme – My hobby: horses. This is a two-colour screen print.

All of the above prints were made using paper stencils.

Creative embroidery

Nowadays there is a reawakening of interest in embroidery. Creative works sometimes combining varieties of fabrics with stitchery are continually being exhibited.

Fig. 9.28
Here we see examples of four pieces of work by Anemone Schneck-Steidl. Her work, much of which is figurative, shows a marvellous use of pattern. The patterns comprise shapes and lines that flow and intermix throughout each piece. All of this work is on a large scale, as is evident in the top right-hand picture.

Embroidery as an exam option

Before starting your embroidery, you will need to refer to your brainstorming list. Make sketches and studies based on your theme, which will have developed considerably since the start of your project. You must collect support studies now, preferably ones that relate to embroidery in its widest sense. Samples of modern hand-embroidered fashion fabrics could be collected.

Fig. 9.29
Grey Geese at Wexford *by Monica Tierney*. *This piece shows a combination of both stitchery and appliqué. The stitches that form the geese contrast well with the textured pattern of stitches in both the shoreline and the sky.*

Fabrics

Any fabric that will allow a needle and thread to pass through it can be considered suitable for embroidery. Finer threads many need to be used on very fine woven fabric, while coarse woven fabric will allow thicker, more chunky threads to be used.

Basic embroidery stitches

Outline stitches

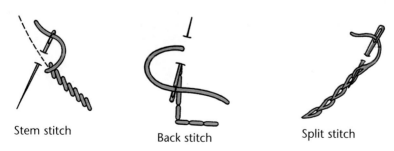

Stem stitch

Back stitch

Split stitch

Fig. 9.30

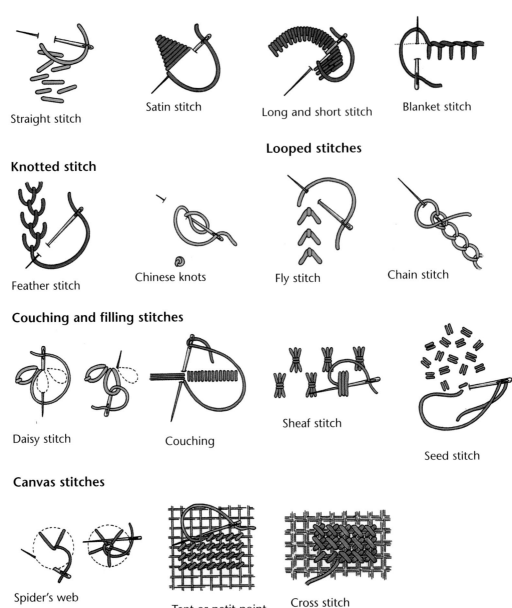

Flat stitches

Straight stitch

Satin stitch

Long and short stitch

Blanket stitch

Knotted stitch

Feather stitch

Chinese knots

Looped stitches

Fly stitch

Chain stitch

Couching and filling stitches

Daisy stitch

Couching

Sheaf stitch

Seed stitch

Canvas stitches

Spider's web

Tent or petit point

Cross stitch

Fig. 9.31

You will need to practise a variety of stitches if you intend to create an embroidery. Only through practice can you achieve fluid stitches of equal size and correct tension. Remember to experiment and create patterns using stitches.

Designing for embroidery

When designing for embroidery, you have to consider whether your work will include stitches only or whether it should also incorporate appliqué. If you use appliqué, a good collection of oddments – buttons, sequins, beads, braids, ribbon, bits of lace, etc. – will be very useful. While much of this can be recycled from old clothing, packets of items suitable for appliqué can be bought in craft and fabric shops.

Materials needed for embroidery

You will need:

- background fabric
- a frame or embroidery hoop – to keep the work stretched while working
- needles – a variety of sizes, some with blunt tips
- threads – a variety of thickness and textures
- a selection of appliqué items
- pins.

Fig. 9.32
A student's embroidery using stitching only, on the theme of buildings and their occupants.

Lino printing

A lino print is a relief print taken from a lino block that has an image cut into its surface.

Designing for lino printing

When designing for a lino print, it is important to have a good contrast of line and texture in your image. Fine delicate lines are best avoided, as they tend to fill with ink and not print well.

Lino blocks can be bought in a variety of sizes from craft shops. A piece about A4 size or a little larger is ideal.

Transferring the design to the block

Make a line drawing of your image on tracing paper. Reverse the tracing paper and trace your image onto the lino block surface. It is important that the traced image is reversed. When this is done, the finished printed image will be facing the correct way.

Fig. 9.33
A three-colour lino print, using one block and an elimination process – that is, continuously cutting away from the same block and overprinting with different colours at each stage of cutting.

Fig. 9.34
A one-colour print.

Both Henri Matisse and Pablo Picasso used lino as a medium for illustrations.

Cutting the lino block

To cut your image onto the lino-block surface, you will need to use lino-cutting tools – small metal gouges, a bit like the nib of a pen, fitted with wooden handles.

Safety

When cutting out lino, always cut away from your body. Keep your fingers well behind the gouge. The instruments are very sharp and accidents can happen easily.

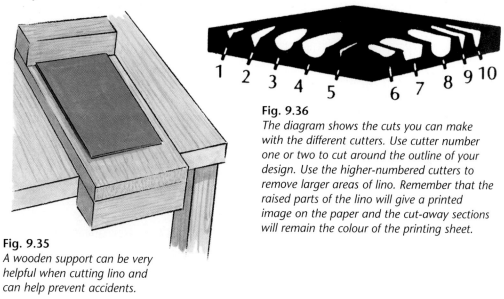

Fig. 9.36
The diagram shows the cuts you can make with the different cutters. Use cutter number one or two to cut around the outline of your design. Use the higher-numbered cutters to remove larger areas of lino. Remember that the raised parts of the lino will give a printed image on the paper and the cut-away sections will remain the colour of the printing sheet.

Fig. 9.35
A wooden support can be very helpful when cutting lino and can help prevent accidents.

Making a print

1. Place ink on a sheet of glass or perspex. You can use oil- or water-based ink, though it is easier to clean up after using water-based inks.
2. Coat a lino roller in the ink and apply it evenly to the lino block.
3. Place a sheet of clean paper over the inked surface.
4. Apply even pressure on the back of the paper. A clean lino roller can be used for this.
5. Gently lift the print off, pulling it from one corner.

More than one colour

There are two methods for making a multi-coloured lino print:

- using a separate block for each colour
- using a process of elimination, using the same block throughout.

Always print from light to dark, that is, applying the lightest colour first.

Fabric printing

Fabric prints can be created using a number of methods. The simplest is to use a stencil (cut from card or special stencil paper) and a stencil brush. This method is very popular for creating borders in rooms, constructed of simple repeat units. This method can also be used to print on fabric. However, a fabric print is usually created by screen printing a repeat pattern onto fabric.

Designing for fabric printing

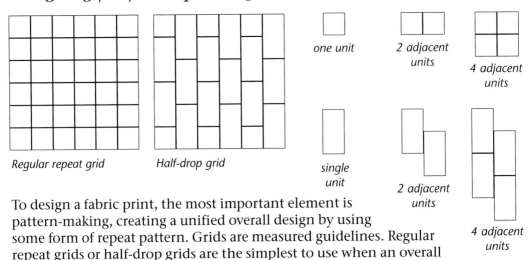

Regular repeat grid   Half-drop grid

one unit

2 adjacent units

4 adjacent units

single unit

2 adjacent units

4 adjacent units

To design a fabric print, the most important element is pattern-making, creating a unified overall design by using some form of repeat pattern. Grids are measured guidelines. Regular repeat grids or half-drop grids are the simplest to use when an overall pattern effect is required.

Overprints are achieved in the same way as for screen printing and the most suitable fabrics for printing are on cotton, polyester cotton, linen and calico. These fabrics absorb the ink well.

Materials needed for fabric printing

You will need:

- a printing bed
- a squeegee
- a screen
- stencil paper or film
- inks
- a fabric marker or needle and thread.

Registration

If you use newsprint stencils for fabric printing, the registration lines can be traced from the original design onto the newsprint. However, the newsprint stencil then needs to be placed against a window or a light box to line the back of the stencil. These lines should correspond exactly to the lines already measured and marked on the fabric.

Print the darkest colours first, if possible. This will help in positioning the screen correctly for subsequent colours, as the dark colour can be seen through the screen.

Fig. 9.37
Registration showing how the repeat-pattern lines on the stencil exactly match the lines on the fabric.

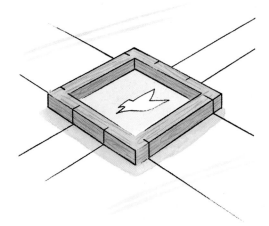

EXAMPLES OF STUDENTS' FABRIC PRINTS

Fig. 9.38

Fig. 9.39

Fig. 9.40

Fig. 9.41

All of these prints are based on the theme of fruit and vegetables and use a half-drop repeat pattern.

10. THE DRAWING EXAM

Drawing from natural or man-made forms and Drawing from the human form

You will most probably have used drawing as a way of producing preparatory work for some parts of your project. If so, you will have had plenty of practice. The purpose of the drawing exam is to test your ability to record and analyse the human figure and either natural or man-made objects.

In creating a drawing, you rely on line and tone to produce a 3D image on your flat sheet of paper. In both drawing exams, tone, composition and proportion (see pages 79, 82–84, 130–31) are the main elements. Tone directly relates to light and how it strikes the subject matter being viewed. The dominant light should come from one direction.

Fig. 10.1
The arrows show the direction of the light.

The *size* of your drawing should be in proportion to your page. Always avoid minute studies.

Texture is the surface quality of an item. It can be rough or smooth. Rough surfaces absorb light, smooth surfaces reflect light.

The human form

The proportions of the human body can be practised and learned.

1. The head is egg-shaped.
2. The widest part of the head is above the temples.
3. The eyes are in the centre and hang from the centre line. The distance between the eyes equals the width of one eye (an eye is one-fifth of the distance across the face).
4. Halfway between the eyes and the end of the chin is the end of the nose.
5. The ears occupy the same space at either side of the face.
6. The mouth is at least the width of the nose, and is nearer the nose than the chin.

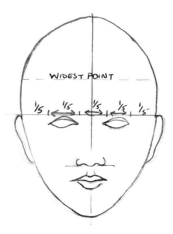

Fig. 10.2
Proportions of the head – front view.

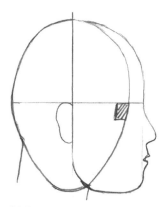

1. The side view of the face resembles an egg with a small section added on.
2. The upper lip cuts through the nostrils. It also projects out further than the lower lip.
3. The eye slopes backwards.
4. The ear begins from the jaw line and occupies the same length as the nose.
5. The end of the nose, the end of the ear and the nape of the neck are in line.
6. The jaw line is usually a square curve.

Fig. 10.3
Proportions of the head – side view.

1. The body is 7.5 times the size of the head (this may vary slightly with each person).
2. The distance across the head is the distance from the neck to the shoulders.
3. The elbows come to the waist.
4. When spread, a hand covers the face.
5. The fingertips reach the middle of the thigh.
6. Limbs get smaller as they go away from the body.
7. The feet are larger than the hands.

Foreshortening

Foreshortening arises when a limb is extended towards the artist, changing the proportion of that limb, making the part that is closest to the artist appear bigger.

The full figure

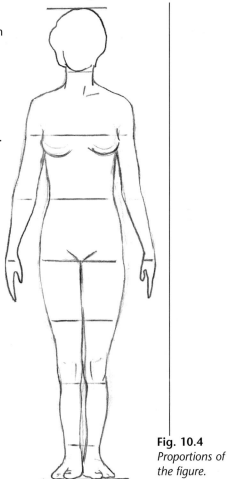

Fig. 10.4
Proportions of the figure.

DRAWING FROM HUMAN FORMS – HEAD AND SHOULDERS

When drawing the human form, work life-size or as large as your page will allow. Concentrate on using a variety of tones to create strong 3D effects.

DRAWING FROM HUMAN FORM –
FULL FIGURE

When drawing the full figure, always indicate the background.

For future reference

Take items from the following lists to practise your observational drawing skills.

Natural forms

- plants, with their various flowers, fruits and seed pods
- fruit and vegetables of all sorts
- bones, driftwood, shells, skulls
- stones
- feathers
- fossils
- root and branch formations
- acorns
- fish, shellfish
- stuffed animals.

Man-made forms

- kitchen utensils
- gardening tools
- woodwork and metalwork tools
- sports equipment
- torches, lamps, lanterns
- decorative objects
- various bags and baskets
- various clothing and accessories
- optical equipment, glasses, binoculars
- radios, cassettes, walkmans, earphones, telephones
- children's toys
- machine parts, clocks
- books, stationery
- drawing equipment
- food and food containers
- bottles, jars, jugs
- firewood and other fuels
- computer equipment.

DRAWING FROM NATURAL FORMS

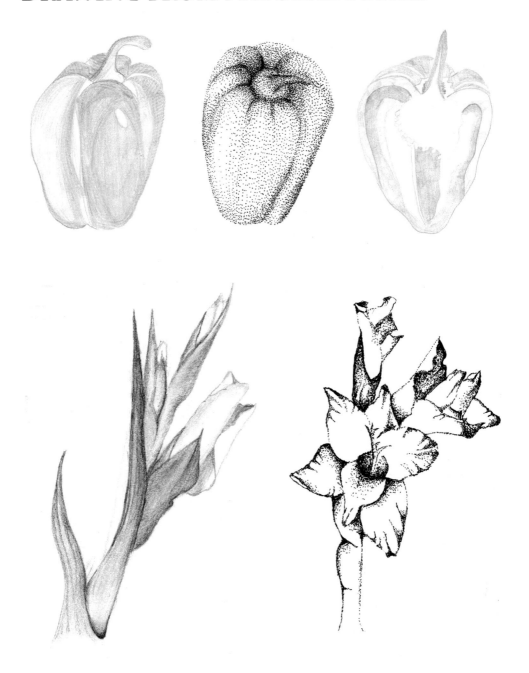

When drawing, experiment with a variety of materials and techniques. In the examples above, both pencil and pen and ink have been used.

DRAWING FROM NATURAL FORMS

Natural forms and man-made forms are sometimes combined, as in the vase with flowers and twigs above.

DRAWING FROM MAN-MADE FORMS

Many man-made forms have a reflective surface which allows for maximum contrast in tone, and makes interesting subject matter for drawing.

DRAWING FROM MAN-MADE FORMS

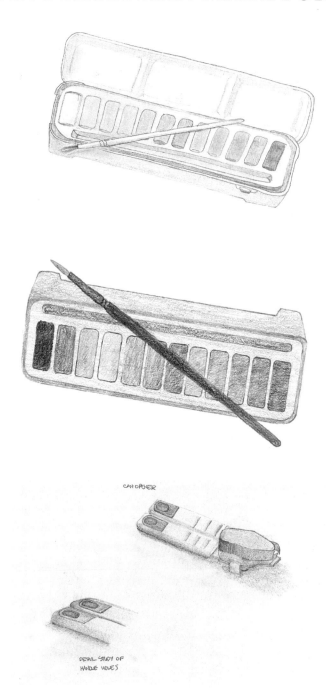

CH OPENER

DETAIL STUDY OF
HANDLE VALVES

In the drawing exam (Higher Level), you are asked to make a drawing of the complete form and a drawing of part of the form that is of particular interest to you.

DRAWING FROM MAN-MADE FORMS

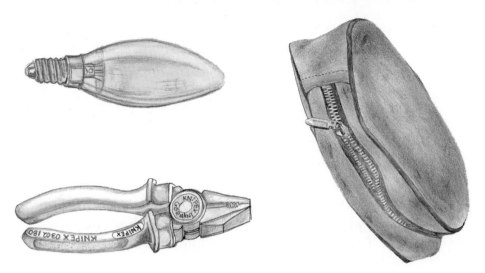

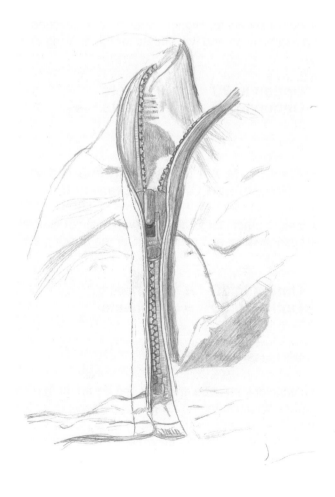

11. GUIDELINES FOR STUDENTS

AN ROINN OIDEACHAIS AGUS EOLAÍOCHTA   BRAINSE NA SCRÚDUITHE BAILE ÁTHA LUAIN

Department of Education and Science   Examinations Branch   Athlone

Teileafón: 0902-74621   Fax: 0902-78562

Guidelines on the contents of the student's Junior Certificate ACD envelope

Junior Certificate Art Craft Design, Higher Level Project and Drawing Examination

The maximum number of sheets for Higher Level must not exceed eleven. This includes the project examination and two sheets for the drawing examination.

> **Option in 2D = 9 sheets**
> **Option in 3D = 8 sheets**

Junior Certificate Art Craft Design, Ordinary Level Project and Drawing Examination

The maximum number of sheets for Ordinary Level must not exceed nine. This includes the project examination and two sheets for the drawing examination.

> **Option in 2D = 7 sheets**
> **Option in 3D = 6 sheets**

(Unlabelled sheets will not be examined.)

The contents of the envelope must be checked and ticked off appropriately. Once the two drawing sheets are placed in the envelope the contents must be updated and ticked off accordingly. The envelope is then sealed and placed with any 3D worked where 3D work exists. 3D work must not be wrapped or packaged.

Instructions to Junior Certificate Art, Craft, Design — Project Candidates

You MAY develop your idea starting from sources of 2D, 3D or Support Studies, working from direct observation or imagination or a combination of both.

PREPARATORY STUDIES are an integral part of the project and must include the candidate's own observed/imagined images. Mere copying/tracing is not accepted.

ENSURE THAT your examination number is clearly shown on all work submitted. Label each of the sheets submitted with the appropriate heading using only the gummed labels to be provided.

ONLY THE required number of A2 sheets (maximum eleven sheets) will be examined. Only one layer of artwork should be placed on each sheet.

DO NOT work on the reverse side of any of these sheets.

Guidelines taken from the Junior Cert. Art Craft Design Syllabus regarding Support Studies.

Support Studies involve History, Critical Appraisal, Evaluation, Appreciation, Science, Technology and correct working vocabulary.

The lessons should be organised as sequential, practical, learning experiences incorporating Drawing and Support Studies as appropriate.

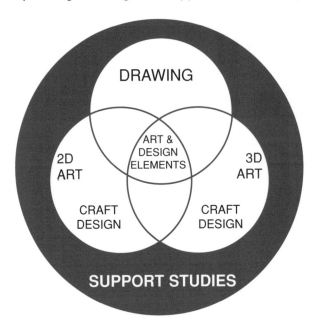

Support Studies

History of Art, Craft and Design should be introduced in relation to the learning experience, with examples from past and present, worldwide as well as local Irish or European work, so as to acquaint the student with adult and child art, craft and design from many cultures. Critical appraisal and evaluation skills should be developed, so as to lead to an understanding and appreciation, as well as enjoyment, of their own work and that of others.

There are certain scientific/mathematical/technological elements in Art, Craft and Design, and these should also be taught as an integral part of each learning experience, as necessary and as they arise.

Art, Craft and Design processes and concepts have a particular vocabulary, and the accurate use of relevant words is crucial to the student's developing grasp of the subject area.

Guidelines taken from the Junior Cert. Art Craft Design Syllabus regarding Painting, Printmaking, Graphic Design and 3D Studies.

PAINTING

Support Studies can provide a lively introduction to painted images from, for example, Egypt, Crete, Russia, medieval and Renaissance European painting, modern American and Irish work. The student should, however, experience the difference between real paintings and reproductions in books or slides, and learn how to enjoy visiting galleries, and to use the public libraries' art, craft and design sections.

PRINTMAKING

Support Studies should include a visit to a printer's, if possible, to exhibitions of prints as well as studying printmaker's images from a number of cultures.

GRAPHIC DESIGN

Support Studies In awakening the student's interests in the whole field of visual communication, the local environment provides examples of graphic design and display in use, e.g. on shopfronts, the sides of vans, newspapers and magazines, road signs.

3D

Support Studies could look at the different types of fine art sculpture, and across the range of functional three-dimensional objects, as in architecture and furnishings. School equipment.

GENERAL LAYOUT AND PRESENTATION OF THE PROJECT

The 2D completed work is straightforward. Just remember to work a bit smaller than the maximum size to allow for labels (titles and numbers) on a backing or mounting sheet.

Fig. 11.1
A well-presented piece of work enhances your project. If possible, get your backing sheet to pick up some of the colours in your work.

Fig. 11.2
If coloured backgrounds are a problem, go for neutral black.

Fig. 11.3
The preparation sheet should include sketches and experiments in composition and techniques.

Measuring, ruling and spacing should be used in order to ensure clarity and neatness. Wait until you are satisfied with your layout before sticking anything down.

Theme: ....
Starting point: ....
Development: ....

Fig. 11.4
Suggested extra label.

- Layout should be clear and pleasing.
- Cut-outs, special mountings, studies and colour experiments should be included.
- Labelling is good as it helps to clarify your ideas.

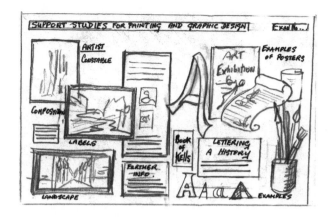

Fig. 11.5
Items may be partly overlapped in your display, but be careful not to cover up important areas.

Magazine cut-outs, postcards, etc. relevant to your project may be used to great effect.

Labelling must be clear (it can be printed or neatly written).

The *background colour* of the mount plays an important part. Keep to one colour, or shades of it, or, alternatively, harmonious colours, for example:

- browns/oranges/reds
- blues and purples
- greens and blues.

Preparation sheets should include examples of sketches (different ideas and studies) and a variety of materials, experiments and techniques (see pages 52–77).

Fig. 11.6
Backing and mounting. If you wish to mount or double-mount some or all of your work, match up your colours and watch your measurements.

Support studies include research and illustrations showing artists' work that connects with your theme/project and other relevant material throughout the book.

Fig. 11.7
Use up to three guidelines for lettering.

Spacing – never go right up to the edge of the paper or page

Clear, readable lettering is essential in your project, so always use guidelines.

Checklist

1. Check that the spacing of words and pictures and/or diagrams is neat and consistent and that it doesn't look as though your display has just been thrown together.
2. Check that straight edges in all cut-out pieces are straight if this is the intention – use a ruler.
3. Check that all spelling is correct.
4. Check that all information is correct.
5. Check that the colours used enhance rather than detract from the information.

12. PAST PROJECTS: HIGHER LEVEL

Coimisiún na Scrúduithe Stáit
State Examinations Commission
JUNIOR CERTIFICATE EXAMINATION 2006

Art Craft Design – *Project*
Higher Level
Issued to Art Teachers & Students of Art, Craft, Design 3rd OCTOBER 2005

Project must be completed by 2nd MAY 2006

Minimum recommended time: 42 hours

300 marks are assigned to the project

- 80 marks – PREPARATION: Research and investigation using a variety of media.
- 80 marks – DEVELOPMENT: Studies showing individual creative ideas.
- 100 marks – REALISATION: The completed 2D and 3D pieces.
- 40 marks – SUPPORT STUDIES: Visual and written relating to project.

THEMES
Candidates will select **ONE**
1. **Keeping Watch**
2. **The Beauty of Change**
3. **At the Table**
4. **Helping Out**
5. **Curiosity**

Instructions to candidates
YOU MAY develop your idea starting from sources of 2D, 3D or Support Studies, working from direct observation or imagination or a combination of both.
PREPARATORY STUDIES are an integral part of the project and must include the candidate's own observed/imagined images. Mere copying/tracing is not accepted.
ENSURE THAT your examination number is clearly shown on all work submitted. Label each of the sheets submitted with the appropriate heading using only the gummed labels to be provided.
ONLY THE required number of A2 sheets (maximum eleven sheets) will be examined.
ONLY ONE layer of artwork should be placed on each sheet.
DO NOT work on the reverse side of any of these sheets.

> ## The Project
> *Required areas of study*
> > **2D studies**
> > **3D studies**
> > **Options**
> > **Support studies**

You may produce the work for the required areas of study in any order you wish. On completion of a work-piece, a selection of the relevant preparatory studies showing the origin and development of the work should be mounted on a sheet of drawing paper 59 cm x 42 cm (A2) maximum dimensions.

2D Studies

> ## *Painting*
> Make a painting based on your starting point.
> Mixed media may be used.

AND

> ## *Graphic Design*
> Design and make one of the following based on your starting point.
> > 1. **Poster**
> > 2. **Video cover**
> > 3. **Book jacket**
> > 4. **Postage stamp**
> > 5. **Record sleeve**
> > 6. **CD cover**
> > 7. **Logo**
> > 8. **Brochure.**

> The maximum size of both the painting and the graphic design must not exceed 59 cm x 42 cm (A2).

Support Studies for 2D

Support studies can be in visual and written form and should relate and reinforce this area of your project. The final selection of these should be mounted on a sheet of paper. Maximum sheet size 59 cm x 42 cm (A2). Only one layer of artwork should be placed on each A2 sheet.

3D Studies

Develop an idea based on your starting point and carry it out in one or any combination of the following:

1. **Modelling**
2. **Carving**
3. **Construction.**

The maximum size of the work-piece must not exceed 80 cm in its largest dimension.

Options

Continue with your chosen starting point as a basis to design and execute **ONE** option of your choice from the following list.

	Maximum size		*Maximum size*
			in any dimension
Batik	59 cm x 42 cm (A2)		
Block Printmaking	59 cm x 42 cm (A2)	**Art Metalwork**	26 cm
Etching	59 cm x 42 cm (A2)	**Carving**	26 cm
Bookcrafts	59 cm x 42 cm (A2)	**Modelling/Casting**	26 cm
Calligraphy	59 cm x 42 cm (A2)	**Packaging**	26 cm
Embroidery	59 cm x 42 cm (A2)	**Pottery/Ceramics**	26 cm
Fabric Printing	59 cm x 42 cm (A2)	**Puppetry**	60 cm
Screen Printing	59 cm x 42 cm (A2)		
Weaving	59 cm x 42 cm (A2)		

It is essential that the maximum dimensions specified for the above options be complied with in each case.

Support Studies for 3D and Options

Support studies can be in visual and written form and should relate and reinforce this area of your project. The final selection of these should be mounted on a sheet of paper. Maximum sheet size 59 cm x 42 cm (A2). Only one layer of artwork should be placed on each A2 sheet.

Checklist for Project at Higher Level

1. **Preparation for painting**

2. **Completed painting**

3. **Preparation for graphic design**

4. **Completed graphic design**

5. **Support studies for painting and graphic design**

6. **Preparation for 3D**

7. **Completed 3D**

8. **Preparation for option (2D or 3D)**

9. **Completed option (2D or 3D)**

10. **Support studies for 3D and option**

Checklist for Drawing Component at Higher Level

11. **Drawing from natural/man-made forms**

12. **Drawing from human forms**

The maximum number of sheets must not exceed eleven. These sheets must be placed in the envelope supplied by the State Examinations Commission. 3D work must be placed on top.

Coimisiún na Scrúduithe Stáit
State Examinations Commission

JUNIOR CERTIFICATE EXAMINATION 2005

Art, Craft, Design – *Project*

Higher Level

Issued to Art Teachers & Students of Art, Craft, Design 5th OCTOBER 2004

Project must be completed by 3rd MAY 2005

Minimum recommended time: 42 hours

300 marks are assigned to the project

80 marks – PREPARATION: Research and investigation using a variety of media.
80 marks – DEVELOPMENT: Studies showing individual creative ideas.
100 marks – REALISATION: The completed 2D and 3D pieces.
40 marks – SUPPORT STUDIES: Visual and written relating to project.

THEMES

Candidates will select **ONE**

1. **Waterside Activity**
2. **All the Fun of the Fair**
3. **Street Market**
4. **Off the Beaten Track**
5. **Development**

Instructions to candidates

SEE PAGES 146–49.

Coimisiún na Scrúduithe Stáit
State Examinations Commission

JUNIOR CERTIFICATE EXAMINATION 2004

Art, Craft, Design – *Project*

Higher Level

Issued to Art Teachers & Students of Art, Craft, Design 6th OCTOBER 2003

Project must be completed by 4th MAY 2004

Minimum recommended time: 42 hours

300 marks are assigned to the project

80 marks – PREPARATION: Research and investigation using a variety of media.
80 marks – DEVELOPMENT: Studies showing individual creative ideas.
100 marks – REALISATION: The completed 2D and 3D pieces.
40 marks – SUPPORT STUDIES: Visual and written relating to project.

THEMES

Candidates will select **ONE**

1. **Waiting**
2. **Night Life**
3. **Exploring**
4. **The Show**
5. **Car Boot Sale**

Instructions to candidates
SEE PAGES 146–49.

Coimisiún na Scrúduithe Stáit
State Examinations Commission

JUNIOR CERTIFICATE EXAMINATION 2003

Art, Craft, Design – *Project*

Higher Level

Issued to Art Teachers & Students of Art, Craft, Design 7th OCTOBER 2002

Project must be completed by 6th **MAY 2003**

Minimum recommended time: 42 hours

300 marks are assigned to the project

  80 marks – PREPARATION: Research and investigation using a variety of media.
  80 marks – DEVELOPMENT: Studies showing individual creative ideas.
100 marks – REALISATION: The completed 2D and 3D pieces.
  40 marks – SUPPORT STUDIES: Visual and written relating to project.

THEMES

Candidates will select **ONE**

1. **My Special Place**
2. **Best Pals**
3. **The Wonders of Nature**
4. **Granny's Collection**
5. **The Things We Take for Granted**
6. **My Favourite Poem or Song**

Instructions to candidates
SEE PAGES 146–49.

An Roinn Oideachais agus Eolaíochta

JUNIOR CERTIFICATE EXAMINATION 2002

Art, Craft, Design – *Project*

Higher Level

Issued to Art Teachers & Students of Art, Craft, Design 11th OCTOBER 2001

Project must be completed by 7th **MAY 2002**

Minimum recommended time: 42 hours

300 marks are assigned to the project

   80 marks – PREPARATION: Research and investigation using a variety of media.
   80 marks – DEVELOPMENT: Studies showing individual creative ideas.
 100 marks – REALISATION: The completed 2D and 3D pieces.
  40 marks – SUPPORT STUDIES: Visual and written relating to project.

THEMES

Candidates will select **ONE**
1. **Pattern in the Landscape/Townscape**
2. **Outside My Door**
3. **Kindness**
4. **Street Life**
5. **My Mama Told Me 'They'd be days like this.'**

Instructions to candidates
SEE PAGES 146–49.

PAST PROJECTS: ORDINARY LEVEL

Coimisiún na Scrúduithe Stáit
State Examinations Commission

JUNIOR CERTIFICATE EXAMINATION 2006

Art, Craft, Design – *Project*

Ordinary Level

Issued to Art Teachers & Students of Art, Craft, Design 3rd OCTOBER 2005

Project must be completed by 2nd MAY 2006

Minimum recommended time: 42 hours

300 marks are assigned to the project

75 marks – PREPARATION: Research and investigation using a variety of media.
75 marks – DEVELOPMENT: Studies showing individual creative ideas.
120 marks – REALISATION: The completed 2D and 3D pieces.
30 marks – SUPPORT STUDIES: Visual and written relating to project.

THEMES

Candidates will select **ONE**
1. **Keeping Watch**
2. **The Beauty of Change**
3. **At the Table**
4. **Helping Out**
5. **Curiosity**

Instructions to candidates

YOU MAY develop your idea starting from sources of 2D, 3D or Support Studies, working from direct observation or imagination or a combination of both.
PREPARATORY STUDIES are an integral part of the project and must include the candidate's own observed/imagined images. Mere copying/tracing is not accepted.
ENSURE THAT your examination number is clearly shown on all work submitted. Label each of the sheets submitted with the appropriate heading using only the gummed labels to be provided.
ONLY THE required number of A2 sheets (maximum eleven sheets) will be examined.
ONLY ONE layer of artwork should be placed on each sheet.
DO NOT work on the reverse side of any of these sheets.

The Project

Required areas of study

2D studies
3D studies
Options
Support studies

You may produce the work for the required areas of study in any order you wish. On completion of a work-piece, a selection of the relevant preparatory studies showing the origin and development of the work should be mounted on a sheet of drawing paper 59 cm x 42 cm (A2) maximum dimensions.

2D Studies

Painting

Make a painting based on your starting point.
Mixed media may be used.

OR

Graphic Design

Design and make one of the following based on your starting point.

1. **Poster**
2. **Video cover**
3. **Book jacket**
4. **Postage stamp**
5. **Record sleeve**
6. **CD cover**
7. **Logo**
8. **Brochure.**

The maximum size of both the painting and the graphic design must not exceed 59 cm x 42 cm (A2).

Support Studies for 2D

Support studies can be in visual and written form and should relate and reinforce this area of your project. The final selection of these should be mounted on a sheet of paper. Maximum sheet size 59 cm x 42 cm (A2). Only one layer of artwork should be placed on each A2 sheet.

3D Studies

Develop an idea based on your starting point and carry it out in one or any combination of the following:

1. **Modelling**
2. **Carving**
3. **Construction.**

The maximum size of the work-piece must not exceed 80 cm in its largest dimension.

Options

Continue with your chosen starting point as a basis to design and execute **ONE** option of your choice from the following list.

	Maximum size		*Maximum size in any dimension*
Batik	59 cm x 42 cm (A2)		
Block Printmaking	59 cm x 42 cm (A2)	**Art Metalwork**	26 cm
Etching	59 cm x 42 cm (A2)	**Carving**	26 cm
Bookcrafts	59 cm x 42 cm (A2)	**Modelling/Casting**	26 cm
Calligraphy	59 cm x 42 cm (A2)	**Packaging**	26 cm
Embroidery	59 cm x 42 cm (A2)	**Pottery/Ceramics**	26 cm
Fabric Printing	59 cm x 42 cm (A2)	**Puppetry**	60 cm
Screen Printing	59 cm x 42 cm (A2)		
Weaving	59 cm x 42 cm (A2)		

It is essential that the maximum dimensions specified for the above options be complied with in each case.

Support Studies for 3D and Options

Support studies can be in visual and written form and should relate and reinforce this area of your project. The final selection of these should be mounted on a sheet of paper. Maximum sheet size 59 cm x 42 cm (A2). Only one layer of artwork should be placed on each A2 sheet.

Checklist for Project at Ordinary Level

| 1. | Preparation for painting or graphic design |

| 2. | Completed painting or graphic design |

| 3. | Support studies for painting or graphic design |

| 4. | Preparation for 3D |

| 5. | Completed 3D |

| 6. | Preparation for option (2D or 3D) |

| 7. | Completed option (2D or 3D) |

| 8. | Support studies for 3D and option |

Checklist for Drawing Component at Ordinary Level

| 9. | Drawing from natural/man-made forms |

| 10. | Drawing from human forms |

The maximum number of sheets must not exceed eleven. These sheets must be placed in the envelope supplied by the State Examinations Commission. 3D work must be placed on top.

Coimisiún na Scrúduithe Stáit
State Examinations Commission

JUNIOR CERTIFICATE EXAMINATION 2005

Art, Craft, Design – *Project*

Ordinary Level

Issued to Art Teachers & Students of Art, Craft, Design 5th OCTOBER 2004

Project must be completed by 3rd MAY 2005

Minimum recommended time: 42 hours

300 marks are assigned to the project

75 marks – PREPARATION: Research and investigation using a variety of media.
75 marks – DEVELOPMENT: Studies showing individual creative ideas.
120 marks – REALISATION: The completed 2D and 3D pieces.
30 marks – SUPPORT STUDIES: Visual and written relating to project.

THEMES

Candidates will select **ONE**

1. **Waterside Activity**
2. **All the Fun of the Fair**
3. **Street Market**
4. **Off the Beaten Track**
5. **Development**

Instructions to candidates

SEE PAGES 154–57.

Coimisiún na Scrúduithe Stáit
State Examinations Commission

JUNIOR CERTIFICATE EXAMINATION 2004

Art, Craft, Design – *Project*

Ordinary Level

Issued to Art Teachers & Students of Art, Craft, Design 6th OCTOBER 2003

Project must be completed by 4th MAY 2004

Minimum recommended time: 42 hours

300 marks are assigned to the project

75 marks – PREPARATION: Research and investigation using a variety of media.
75 marks – DEVELOPMENT: Studies showing individual creative ideas.
120 marks – REALISATION: The completed 2D and 3D pieces.
30 marks – SUPPORT STUDIES: Visual and written relating to project.

THEMES

Candidates will select **ONE**

1. **Waiting**
2. **Night Life**
3. **Exploring**
4. **The Show**
5. **Car Boot Sale**

Instructions to candidates

SEE PAGES 154–57.

An Roinn Oideachais agus Eolaíochta

JUNIOR CERTIFICATE EXAMINATION 2003

Art, Craft, Design – *Project*

Ordinary Level

Issued to Art Teachers & Students of Art, Craft, Design 7th OCTOBER 2002

Project must be completed by 6th MAY 2003

Minimum recommended time: 42 hours

300 marks are assigned to the project

- 75 marks – PREPARATION: Research and investigation using a variety of media.
- 75 marks – DEVELOPMENT: Studies showing individual creative ideas.
- 120 marks – REALISATION: The completed 2D and 3D pieces.
- 30 marks – SUPPORT STUDIES: Visual and written relating to project.

THEMES

Candidates will select **ONE**

1. **My Special Place**
2. **Best Pals**
3. **The Wonders of Nature**
4. **Granny's Collection**
5. **The Things We Take for Granted**
6. **My Favourite Poem or Song**

Instructions to candidates

See pages 154–57.

An Roinn Oideachais agus Eolaíochta

JUNIOR CERTIFICATE EXAMINATION 2002

Art, Craft, Design – *Project*

Ordinary Level

Issued to Art Teachers & Students of Art, Craft, Design 11th OCTOBER 2001

Project must be completed by 7th MAY 2002

Minimum recommended time: 42 hours

300 marks are assigned to the project

75 marks – PREPARATION: Research and investigation using a variety of media.
75 marks – DEVELOPMENT: Studies showing individual creative ideas.
120 marks – REALISATION: The completed 2D and 3D pieces.
30 marks – SUPPORT STUDIES: Visual and written relating to project.

THEMES

Candidates will select **ONE**

1. **Pattern in the Landscape/Townscape**
2. **Outside My Door**
3. **Kindness**
4. **Street Life**
5. **My Mama Told Me 'They'd be days like this.'**

Instructions to candidates

SEE PAGES 154–57.

13. PAST DRAWING EXAMS: HIGHER LEVEL

■ The drawing examination will take place in May. You should receive the question paper seven days prior to this examination.

■ During these seven days you may practise drawing your chosen item from EITHER Category A (Natural Forms) *or* Category B (Man Made Forms), from the Examination Paper.

■ You may also practise drawing the described prose in Category C (Human Forms) from the Examination Paper.

■ On the day of the Examination you must begin your drawings on blank, empty drawing sheets.

■ NO ARTWORK OF ANY KIND MUST ACCOMPANY YOU INTO THE EXAMINATION CENTRE.

NOTE: STUDENTS MAY TAKE ITEMS FROM THE LISTS ON PAGE 134 ('For future reference') TO PRACTISE THEIR OBSERVATIONAL DRAWING SKILLS.

Coimisiún na Scrúduithe Stáit
State Examinations Commission

JUNIOR CERTIFICATE EXAMINATION 2005

Art, Craft, Design – *Project*
Higher Level

Issued to Art Teachers & Students of Art, Craft, Design 27th APRIL 2005

100 MARKS ARE ASSIGNED TO THIS PAPER

Examination takes place on 4th MAY 2005

Instructions to candidates

You ARE allowed to use colour if you wish and any suitable media: Pencils, Pastels, Crayons, Pen and Ink, Paints, Markers, or any combination of these, to create your drawings.

DRAWING SHEETS must not exceed A2 size.

PLEASE ENSURE that you have your correct examination number clearly shown in the space provided on all submitted drawing sheets.

THE NATURAL Forms and Man Made Forms examinations will both begin at 9.30 am and end at 10.30 am.

THERE WILL be an interval of 20 minutes' duration between the end of your first choice examination and the commencement of the Human Forms examination, which will begin at 11.00 am and end at 12.30 pm.

THE TIME allowed for the drawing of Human Forms is 90 minutes, which includes all rest periods for the live model.

DURING THE examination, the superintendent will return to you the State Examinations Commission envelope containing your 2D project work. When all sections of this examination are completed, place your drawings in the envelope along with the rest of your project work.

THEN SEAL the envelope.

You are required to make a study from:

Category A	Natural Forms	9.30 am–10.30 am
OR		
Category B	Man Made Forms	9.30 am–10.30 am
AND ALSO FROM		
Category C	Human Forms	11.00 am–12.30 pm

Category A
MARKS–OBSERVATION 25   INTERPRETATION 25

Natural Forms
Choose one from the list below
> **Apple**
> **Banana**
> **Ferns/bracken**
> **Firewood**
> **Flower/shrub**
> **Lettuce**
> **Lichen**
> **Orange**
> **Potato**
> **Stones/pebbles**
> **Tree branch**

Make a drawing of the complete form _and_ also a drawing of a part of it which appeals to you. This part may be enlarged in order to emphasise all its features.

Or

Category B
MARKS–OBSERVATION 25   INTERPRETATION 25

Man Made Forms
Choose one from the list below

Bag/basket
Belt/buckle
Book
Computer mouse
Egg carton
Hairbrush/dryer
Sunglasses
Shoe
Torch
Umbrella
Watch/clock

Make a drawing of the complete form *and* also a drawing of a part of it which appeals to you. This part may be enlarged in order to emphasise all its features.

Category C
MARKS–OBSERVATION 25   INTERPRETATION 25

Human Forms
The required live pose

The live model provided for this examination should be seated on a chair.

The model's knees should be bent, with left foot resting on the floor, and right leg crossed over left leg, at the knee.

The model's right hand should be holding a glass which is resting on top of left hand.

Both arms in a relaxed position, head turned to the right.

You are required to make a drawing of the live model showing the complete pose
or
You are required to make a drawing of the live model showing the head and shoulders. All facial features visible to you must be recorded in your drawing.

PAST DRAWING EXAMS: ORDINARY LEVEL

- The drawing examination will take place in May. You should receive the question paper seven days prior to this examination.
- During these seven days you may practise drawing your chosen item from EITHER Category A (Natural Forms) or Category B (Man Made Forms), from the Examination Paper.
- You may also practise drawing the described prose in Category C (Human Forms) from the Examination Paper.
- On the day of the Examination you must begin your drawings on blank, empty drawing sheets.
- NO ARTWORK OF ANY KIND MUST ACCOMPANY YOU INTO THE EXAMINATION CENTRE.

NOTE: STUDENTS MAY TAKE ITEMS FROM THE LISTS ON PAGE 134 ('For future reference') TO PRACTISE THEIR OBSERVATIONAL DRAWING SKILLS.

Coimisiún na Scrúduithe Stáit
State Examinations Commission

JUNIOR CERTIFICATE EXAMINATION 2005

Art, Craft, Design – *Project*
Ordinary Level

Issued to Art Teachers & Students of Art, Craft, Design 27th APRIL 2005

100 MARKS ARE ASSIGNED TO THIS PAPER

Examination takes place on 4th MAY 2005

Instructions to candidates

You ARE allowed to use colour if you wish and any suitable media: Pencils, Pastels, Crayons, Pen and Ink, Paints, Markers, or any combination of these, to create your drawings.

DRAWING SHEETS must not exceed A2 size.

PLEASE ENSURE that you have your correct examination number clearly shown in the space provided on all submitted drawing sheets.

THE NATURAL Forms and Man Made Forms examinations will both begin at 9.30 am and end at 10.30 am.

THERE WILL be an interval of 20 minutes' duration between the end of your first choice examination and the commencement of the Human Forms examination, which will begin at 11.00 am and end at 12.30 pm.

THE TIME allowed for the drawing of Human Forms is 90 minutes, which includes all rest periods for the live model.

DURING THE examination, the superintendent will return to you the State Examinations Commission envelope containing your 2D project work. When all sections of this examination are completed, place your drawings in the envelope along with the rest of your project work.

THEN SEAL the envelope.

You are required to make a study from:

Category A	Natural Forms	9.30 am–10.30 am
OR		
Category B	Man Made Forms	9.30 am–10.30 am
AND ALSO FROM		
Category C	Human Forms	11.00 am–12.30 pm

Category A
MARKS–OBSERVATION 25   INTERPRETATION 25

Natural Forms
Choose one from the list below

- **Apple**
- **Banana**
- **Ferns/bracken**
- **Firewood**
- **Flower/shrub**
- **Lettuce**
- **Lichen**
- **Orange**
- **Potato**
- **Stones/pebbles**
- **Tree branch**

Make a drawing of the complete form *and* also a drawing of a part of it which appeals to you. This part may be enlarged in order to emphasise all its features.

Or

Category B

MARKS–OBSERVATION 25   INTERPRETATION 25

Man Made Forms

Choose one from the list below

> **Bag/basket**
> **Belt/buckle**
> **Book**
> **Computer mouse**
> **Egg carton**
> **Hairbrush/dryer**
> **Sunglasses**
> **Shoe**
> **Torch**
> **Umbrella**
> **Watch/clock**

Make a drawing of the complete form *and* also a drawing of a part of it which appeals to you. This part may be enlarged in order to emphasise all its features.

Category C

MARKS–OBSERVATION 25   INTERPRETATION 25

Human Forms

The required live pose

> **The live model provided for this examination should be seated on a chair.**
>
> **The model's knees should be bent, with left foot resting on the floor, and right leg crossed over left leg, at the knee.**
>
> **The model's right hand should be holding a glass which is resting on top of left hand.**
>
> **Both arms in a relaxed position, head turned to the right.**

You are required to make a drawing of the live model showing the complete pose
or
You are required to make a drawing of the live model showing the head and shoulders. All facial features visible to you must be recorded in your drawing.

14. USEFUL VOCABULARY FOR YOUR PROJECT

Abstract art	A non-naturalistic representation of a subject. In abstract art, colour, line, pattern, shape and tone are more important in their own right than the subject matter or object being represented.
Aesthetic	A sense of beauty and quality within a work.
Asymmetrical balance	Based on equal eye attraction or visual weight. A large object near the centre of gravity is balanced by a smaller object further away.

Background	See pages 82–3.
Canvas	A heavy fabric usually woven from cotton or linen, which is stretched onto a wooden frame and primed to make the surface suitable for painting.
Chalk drawing	A drawing which is produced using pastel or conte as a drawing medium.
Charcoal	A black charred wood sold in drawing sticks of different thicknesses. It has a powdery quality and a charcoal drawing needs to be sprayed with fixative to stop it from smudging.
Collage	A French word which means 'paste up'. An arrangement or composition made up of pieces of torn or cut paper, or other materials.
Complementary colours	Colours which are directly opposite each other on the colour wheel, for example, red and green, orange and blue, yellow and purple.
Composition	See pages 82–4.
Conte	Conte are synthetic chalks which have a fine texture.
Contrast	The difference between two things, for example, black and white, hot and cold, happy and sad, etc.
Cool colours	Associated with the sea, usually blues, greens and violets.

Cross-hatching	See page 80.
Cubism	An art movement, led by Picasso and Braque, that began in France in the early 1900s. The Cubist artists simplified all forms to geometric shapes. Many sides of their chosen subject were shown in a piece of work.
Distortion	To twist out of shape – a technique which was used by the Cubists and the Surrealists.
Drawing	See pages 80, 130–31.
Eye-level	See page 85.
Fantasy	See pages 39–41.
Fixative	A substance sprayed onto charcoal, conte, pastel pencil or chalk drawings to prevent them from smudging.
Focal point	See pages 84–5.
Foreground	See pages 82–3.
Format	See page 81.
Fresco	A fresco is a painting applied to a freshly plastered surface (usually a wall) while the plaster is still wet. The paint soaks in as the plaster dries.
Genre	Scenes from everyday life, a popular movement in Holland in the seventeenth century – Vermeer's paintings are a fine example.
Gouache	A type of paint often used in graphic work because it gives an even, opaque finish.
Harmonious colours	Colours that work well together aesthetically. They are usually found next to each other on the colour wheel. Tints or shades of any colour are also harmonious.
Highlight	This word may be used in two ways: the first describes the memorable part of a picture; the second a bright spot in a picture.
Horizon line	See page 85.
Impressionism	A movement in painting towards the end of the nineteenth century, in which the artists, the Impressionists, experimented with colour and light.

Landscapes/seascapes	Paintings based on scenic views of nature. Until the sixteenth century, landscapes and seascapes were used to fill the backgrounds of paintings. Constable and Turner were responsible for making landscapes and seascapes popular subjects in the eighteenth and nineteenth centuries.
Light source	See page 130.
Medium	The material in which the artist works, for example, oil paint, watercolour, chalk, pencil, stone, metal, clay, plaster, etc.
Method	A way of working.
Mid-ground	See pages 81–2.
Mount	See pages 78, 144–5.
Mythological painting	Based on the myths of the gods and heroes of ancient Greece and Rome.
Naturalism	The accurate and faithful representation of objects in every detail, as they appear in front of you.
Observation	Meaning 'studying visually' – usually used in the context of still life or the drawing or painting of an object.
Oil paint	Paint made from pigment mixed with oil (usually linseed oil). The paint is diluted with turpentine or white spirit.
One-point perspective	See page 85.
Painterly	A style in which pictures are made with colour, tone, light and shade, rather than with lines, as in drawing.
Pastel	Opaque sticks of pigment. Manufactured in both chalk and oil. Chalk pastels need to be fixed to prevent them from smudging.
Pencil	A pencil contains a form of carbon (graphite) in a wooden casing. Pencils are used for drawing and make different kinds of marks according to their degree of hardness or softness.
Perspective	See page 85.
Plen-air	Painting which is executed out of doors rather than in the studio. The Impressionists were plen-air artists.

Pointillism	A neo-Impressionist technique of applying paint in small dots of pure colour that blend optically when viewed from a distance, normally taken to be three times the diameter of the canvas.
Preparatory work	See page 7, and throughout the book.
Realism	Painting or drawing exactly what is in front of you. Some artists are so painstakingly precise in their painting that they are called photorealists.
Secondary colour	Produced when two primary colours are mixed together. The secondary colours are orange, green and purple.
Shading	The introduction of tonal areas into a drawing, creating a 3D effect on a 2D surface.
Sketch	A quick drawing which is often used as the preparatory work for a more finished piece.
Space	The distance between places or objects.
Support studies	See page 142.
Surrealism	An art movement founded by André Breton in 1924. Surrealist work has a dream-like quality that incorporates fantasy.
Texture	Surface quality, that is, the degree of roughness or smoothness.
Tint	A colour as it moves towards white.
2D	An abbreviation for 'two-dimensional', the two dimensions being length and breath. The surface of a sheet of paper is 2D, therefore creating 3D images on a sheet of paper is illusory.
Vanishing point	See page 85.
Warm colours	Associated with fire, mostly reds, oranges and yellows.
Wash	A thin mixture of paint, used to cover a surface evenly, or graded – light to dark or dark to light.

ACKNOWLEDGMENTS

The authors wish to thank the students, and their teachers, who have allowed samples of projects to be reproduced in this book on an anonymous basis.

For permission to reproduce photographs and works of art, grateful acknowledgment is made to the following:

Image File pp.8 (top), 9 (top), 19, 23 (top), 30 (top left and right), 39, 40 (bottom left), 42, 46 (all), 47 (all), 48, 51 (top).

Corbis pp.21 (bottom), 23 (bottom), 24 (top left), 82 (both).

Associated Press pp.29, 105.

Leenane by Paul Henry (p.8), photograph reproduced with the kind permission of The Trustees of the Museums & Galleries of Northern Ireland.

Yellow Bungalow by Gerard Dillon (p.9), photograph reproduced with the kind permission of The Trustees of the Museums & Galleries of Northern Ireland, © the artist.

Bedroom at Ballylough by Arthur Charlton Armstrong (p.14), photograph reproduced with the kind permission of The Trustees of the Museums & Galleries of Northern Ireland, © Mr H. Greenaway.

Medical Students by Gerard Dillon (p.14), photograph reproduced with the kind permission of The Trustees of the Museums & Galleries of Northern Ireland, © the artist.

The Discussion by Renato Guttuso (p.16) courtesy of The Tate, London, © DACS 2002.

The Shelter Warden by Thomas A. Crawley (p.17), photograph reproduced with the kind permission of The Trustees of the Museums & Galleries of Northern Ireland.

The Execution of the Rebels on the 3rd of May by Francisco Goya (p.17) courtesy of The Art Archive/Museo del Prado, Madrid.

WHAAM! by Roy Lichtenstein (p.17) courtesy of The Tate, London, © The Estate of Roy Lichtenstein/DACS 2002.

A Fight (c.1935) by L.S. Lowry (p.18) printed by permission of The Lowry Collection, Salford.

Freedom of Speech (p.18), *Rosie the Riveter* (p.18) and *Freedom from Want* (p.45) by Norman Rockwell printed by permission of The Norman Rockwell Family Agency Copyright © 2002 the Norman Rockwell Family Agency.

Rib of Beef by Gustave Caillebotte (p.20) courtesy of The Art Institute of Chicago.

Les Joueurs de Cartes by Paul Cézanne (p.22) courtesy of Musée d'Orsay, Paris, legacy of the Count Isaac de Camondo, 1911.

Light Falls Within by Carol Graham (p.23), photograph reproduced with the kind permission of The Trustees of the Museums & Galleries of Northern Ireland, © the artist.

La Liseuse by Mary Cassatt (p.24) courtesy of SuperStock.

Vanessa Bell by Duncan Grant (p.24) © 1978, Estate of Duncan Grant, courtesy of Henrietta Garnett/NPG London.

The Red Hammock by Sir John Lavery (p.24), photograph reproduced with the kind permission of The Trustees of the Museums & Galleries of Northern Ireland, and by courtesy of Felix Rosenstiel's Widow & Son Ltd., London on behalf of the Estate of Sir John Lavery.

The Girl in the Window by Harry Morley (p.24) courtesy of Christie's Images, London and SuperStock.

Cat On Mat by Jack Hanlon (p.25) courtesy of The National Gallery of Ireland, © the artist's estate.

A Couple of Foxhounds by George Stubbs (p.25) courtesy of The Tate, London.

For The Road by Jack Yeats (p.26) courtesy of The National Gallery of Ireland, © Michael Yeats.

Mares and Foals in a River Landscape by George Stubbs (pp.27, 83) courtesy of The Tate, London.

Race Horses at the Grandstand by Edgar Degas (p.27) courtesy of Musée d'Orsay, Paris.

The Blank Signature by René Magritte (p.27) courtesy of The Board of Trustees, National Gallery of Art, Washington, © ADAGP, Paris and DACS, London 2002.

Knight, Death and Devil by Albrecht Dürer (p.28) courtesy of The Board of Trustees, National Gallery of Art, Washington.

Death on a Pale Horse – The Fourth of the Apocalypse by William Blake (p.28) courtesy of Fitzwilliam Museum, Cambridge.

Stamps by Joe Dunne (p.30) and Charles Rycraft (p.51) reproduced by kind permission of An Post ©.

La Ferme de Lézavier, Finistére by Roderic O'Conor (p.33) courtesy of The National Gallery of Ireland, © the artist's estate.

Dorset Chalk Quarry by Harry N. Morley (p.33) courtesy of Christie's Images, London and SuperStock.

Two Calla Lilies on Pink by Georgia O'Keeffe (p.34) courtesy of Philadelphia Museum of Art: Bequest of Georgia O'Keeffe for the Alfred Stieglitz Collection, 1987, © ARS, NY and DACS, London 2002.

Flowers by Jack Hanlon (p.34) courtesy of Hugh Lane Gallery, Dublin, © the artist's estate.

Three Cats by Elizabeth Blackadder (p.35) © the artist.

Studies of Cats by John Ward (p.35) © the artist.

Detail from *Cape Cod Evening* by Edward Hopper (p.35) courtesy of The Board of Trustees, National Gallery of Art, Washington.

Three Dancers by Pablo Picasso (p.36) courtesy of The Tate, London, © Succession Picasso/DACS 2002.

Cellomaster by Arman (p.37) courtesy of Hugh Lane Gallery, Dublin, © ADAGP, Paris and DACS, London 2002.

Portrait of a Young Woman by Meredith Frampton (p.37) © Tate, London 2002.

Quintette by Raoul Dufy (p.37) courtesy of Christie's Images, London and SuperStock, © ADAGP, Paris and DACS, London 2002.

Watching TV by Tsing-Fang Chen (p.38) courtesy of Lucia Gallery, New York City, TF Chen/SuperStock.

Modern Madonna by Christian Pierre (p.38) courtesy of Private Collection/Christian Pierre/SuperStock.

Elohim Creating Adam by William Blake (p.40) courtesy of The Tate, London.

Les Amants by René Magritte (p.40) courtesy of The Art Archive/Dagli Orti, Paris, © ADAGP, Paris and DACS, London 2002.

The Lament for Icarus by Herbert J. Draper (p.40) courtesy of The Tate, London.

La Decouverte Du Feu (p.40) by René Magritte © ADAGP, Paris and DACS, London 2002.

Design for the Red House by E.W. Godwin (p.43) courtesy of V&A Picture Library.

Notre Dame Du Haut at Ronchamp by Le Corbusier (p.44) © FLC.

Long-term Parking by Arman (p.49) © ADAGP, Paris and DACS, London 2002.

Universal Hearse (p.49) courtesy of Todd Ramquist.

The Arrival by Christopher Nevinson (p.50) © Tate, London 2002.

Barge at Edenderry by Romeo Charles Toogood (p.50), photograph reproduced with the kind permission of The Trustees of the Museums & Galleries of Northern Ireland, © the artist's estate.

Night Train by Paul Delvaux (p.51) Musées royaux des Beaux-Arts de Belgique courtesy of © Foundation P Delvaux, St Idesbald, Belgium/DACS, London 2002.

La Madeleine a La Veilleuse by Georges de la Tour (p.83) courtesy of The Art Archive/Musée du Louvre, Paris/Dagli Orti, Paris.

The Magpie by Claude Monet (p.83) courtesy of The Art Archive/Musée d'Orsay, Paris/Dagli Orti, Paris.

Still Life by Pieter Claesz (p.86) courtesy of The National Gallery of Ireland.

Composition (1929) by Piet Mondrian (p.86) courtesy of the Solomon R. Guggenheim Museum, New York, © Piet Mondrian 2002 Mondrian/Holtzman Trust c/o Beeldrecht, Hoofddorp & DACS, London.

Wheat Fields with Sheaves by Vincent van Gogh (p.86) courtesy of Honolulu Academy of Arts, Hawaii/SuperStock.

Victor Bicycles poster by W.H. Bradley (p.87) courtesy of V&A Picture Library.

Saturday Night Fever – The Musical poster (p.87, 94) courtesy of Dewynters, London, © The Robert Stigwood Organisation.

Grease poster (p.87) courtesy of Dewynters, London, © The Robert Stigwood Organisation.

Unicef (p.87) The UNICEF emblem and name are the exclusive property of UNICEF. They are protected under international law. Unauthorised use is prohibited. They may not be copied or reproduced in any way without the prior written permission of UNICEF.

Toy Train and Airplane Stamp (p.87) © Consignia plc 1989. Reproduced by kind permission of Consignia. All rights reserved.

Leicester Galleries poster by Anne C. Patterson (p.95) courtesy of V&A Picture Library.

Metropolis poster by Schulz-Neudamm (p.95) courtesy of Digital Image © 2002 The Museum of Modern Art/Scala, Florence.

Feel the Buzz but you don't need Drugs poster (p.95) courtesy of the Department of Health and Children, Dublin.

Leicester Galleries poster by Paul Nash (p.95) courtesy of V&A Picture Library.

Picture This! (p.96) courtesy of Hugh Lane Gallery, Dublin © Aidan Hickey.

National Print Museum, Dublin (p.101).

By Swerve of Shore by Michael Fewer (p.97), jacket design by Slick Fish Design, photography by Michael Fewer.

Little Dancer Aged Fourteen by Edgar Degas (p.106) courtesy of The Tate, London.

Rainbow over Baltimore, Co. Cork (p.114), *Christmas in St Patrick's Cathedral, Dublin* (p.115) and detail from *Thatched House near Ardmore* (p.115) by Bernadette Madden © the artist.

Four tapestries from *Textilkunst* by Anemone Schneck-Steidl (p.122) © the artist.

Grey Geese at Wexford by Monica Tierney (p.123) © the artist.